Presented to:

Trey

Presented by:

Date:

1-3 02/4

E-mail from God for Kids

by
Claire Cloninger and Andy Cloninger

RIVER
OAK
PUBLISHING

Tulsa, Oklahoma

E-mail from God for Kids
ISBN 1-58919-996-0
Copyright © 2001 by Claire Cloninger and
Andy Cloninger
Represented by: Alive Communications, Inc.
7680 Goddard Street
Suite 200
Colorado Springs, CO 80920

Published by RiverOak Publishing
P.O. Box 700143
Tulsa, OK 74170-0143

Claire's Dedication

This book is dedicated to the memory of my
sister, Alix, and to the "kids"
and grandkids who loved her: Paul, Jeanne,
Andre´, and Marc; Jacob, Gabriel,
Matthew, Mary Grace, Beau, and Nicholas.

Andy's Dedication

This book is also dedicated to the kids at
Spanish Fort United Methodist,
Christ Church Mobile (Anglican), and
Young Life Mobile.

Introduction

Have you ever opened your eyes on Sunday morning and thought to yourself, *Well, I guess I have to get up and go to church. Boring?* Listen. If you knew God as He really is, you'd realize that He's anything but boring. God is not some white-bearded old guy in a stained-glass window. He's real! He's alive! He's more awesome, more amazing, and more dynamic than anyone you've ever known. He is mind-blowing. He is a total trip.

God knows every person who's ever been created. No wonder. He's the one who created them—all of them, including you!

God knows you so well it would surprise you. He knows what you're thinking right now. He knows what you're feeling, what makes you laugh, and what makes you cry. He knows you backwards, forwards, and inside out; and He's crazy about you! That's why He wants to spend time with you. He wants you to know him too.

E-Mail from God for Kids speaks God's words in everyday language. It is full of good news, hope, help, encouragement, and love. It gives real answers to real problems. This is your chance to log on to God's heart and mind. So what are you waiting for?

Claire Cloninger

EVERYDAY FAITH

Then Jesus told him, "Because you have seen me, you have believed; blessed are those who have not seen and yet have believed."

| John | 20:29 |

My child,

>You may not realize it, but faith is something you use every day. If you get into the car with your parents to go to the mall, you don't sit there the whole trip and say, "Maybe we'll get there; maybe we won't." No, you just assume that if you're heading to the mall, then you'll get to the mall. You trust in what you can see, like the driver, the road, and the car. But you also trust in things you can't see. You trust that other drivers won't smash into you, that a part of the engine won't fall out, that a tree won't fall right in your way. That's everyday faith, and everybody has it.

You can use this same kind of faith to believe in me. I'm not totally unseen. You see me in nature's beauty, in miraculous things that happen around you every day, and in the Bible. But you will have to learn to use your faith to trust me in ways you can't see me—like physically.

The disciples saw Jesus in the flesh and believed. But you are even more blessed when you believe with your faith.

The One You Can Believe In,

God

=== =========

E-mail from God for Kids

Can a mother forget [her] baby ... and have
no compassion on the child she has borne?
Though she may forget, I will not forget you!

| Isaiah | 49:15 |

Dear Child,

>No matter what your parents are like, they won't ever be perfect. Sometimes they will forget about what's important to you. Sometimes they won't understand what you want them to understand. But you have a heavenly Parent who is perfect in every way.

I'm your perfect Parent. I love you with a love that never makes a mistake. I always see what you need and understand how you feel. When the people in your life aren't perfect, you can turn to me. I'll be here to understand you and help you. I'll help you respect your parents, even when they make mistakes. And I will love you with my perfect love.

Your Heavenly Parent,

God

=== =========

FORGET ABOUT BEING COOL

*I tell you the truth, anyone who will
not receive the kingdom of God like a little
child will never enter it.*

	Mark	10:15	

Dear Child of Mine,

>Do you ever feel like everything in the world is telling you to grow up before you are ready? Well, I'm telling you just the opposite. Keep a childlike heart and a childlike attitude. People who get too cool and "grown up" will never feel at home in my kingdom.

What does it mean to have a childlike heart and attitude? You know how little children are always ready to trust their parents? I want you to trust me like that. You know how little kids are excited about life? I want you to have that same kind of excitement.

Trust me, believe me, and have fun in your life. Forget about being cool.

Father of the Childlike Heart,

God

=== =========

E-mail from God for Kids

This hope we have as an anchor of the soul,
a hope both sure and steadfast and one
which enters within the veil.

Hebrews   6:19 NASB

My child,

>You can ride on a big boat and never miss the anchor until you want to stop and stay in one spot. When you're speeding around from place to place, you may not even notice that the anchor is missing. But when it comes time to be still for a while, you need an anchor to keep the boat from drifting. Or when a storm blows up and you want to anchor in deep water and ride it out, you can't do that without an anchor.

It's easy to rush around in life and never even know what it is to be quiet. But there is a longing in every person for stillness and peace. There is a need in every person for security in the storms of life. I want to be your anchor. I want to give you the peace to sit still and rest. I want to give you the security to ride out life's wild storms. I am here for you. Let me anchor your life to my love.

Your Anchor,

God

=== ==========

MAKE THE CHOICE

If you confess with your mouth Jesus as Lord, and believe in your heart that God raised Him from the dead, you will be saved; for with the heart a person believes, resulting in righteousness, and with the mouth he confesses, resulting in salvation.

  Romans **10:9–10** NASB

My Child,

>I'm not going to make you believe in me. That's a choice you'll have to make for yourself. I don't want a bunch of brainwashed, robotic Christians who love me because they have to. I want my children to make their own decision to choose me and follow me.

I've given you all the tools you need to make that decision for yourself. I gave you the Bible to read and understand me. I gave you an incredible world to show you my beauty. I sent Jesus Christ to show you the way to me. I gave you the Holy Spirit to guide you on the path to me. But only you can take all of that stuff and make a decision to follow me.

So seek the truth; learn all you can; and then make up your own mind. I love you so much, and I want you to choose me. But I'm not going to force you.

Your Father,

God

=== =========

E-mail from God for Kids

*I can do everything through him
who gives me strength.*

	Philippians	4:13	

My Child,

>Every person who has ever done anything great, from climbing a mountain to creating a sculpture, began with a dream. I want to put huge dreams and plans in your heart. I want to show you great things you can do with your life. I want to use you to make a difference in the world.

When I give you a dream, never think of it as something you'll have to do all by yourself. Whatever I ask you to do, I'll be doing it with you. I'll give you the strength and the brains and the energy you will need to get the job done. If you end up building huge skyscrapers, I'll be building them with you. If you decide to be a world traveler, I'll travel with you. If you travel through space as an astronaut, I'll be along for the ride. So dream big and believe in your future. You can count on my strength.

Your Helper,

God

=== =========

A VERY IMPORTANT QUESTION

"But what about you?" he asked.
"Who do you say I am?" Peter answered,
"You are the Christ."

| Mark | 8:29 |

My Child,

>Once, Jesus asked his friends what people were saying about him. Peter told Jesus that some people were saying he was John the Baptist come back to life, and other people were saying he was a prophet. Then Jesus asked Peter a very important question. "But what about you?" he asked. "Who do *you* say that I am?"

Now I want to ask you that question. Who do you say that Jesus is? Don't take the word of other kids. Don't just trust teachers to tell you. They might not know. Read about Jesus in the Bible. Pray to him and ask him to be your Savior. Then see how he can change your life. You'll find out who Jesus is by looking for him.

His Father and Yours,

God

=== =========

E-mail from God for Kids

All men are like grass, and all their glory is like the flowers of the field.... The grass withers and the flowers fall, but the word of our God stands forever.

Isaiah	40:6-8

Dear Child of Mine,

>Who are the most powerful people in the world? Are they movie stars? Athletes? Rock stars? Whoever they are, in time their power will fade away, and they will disappear from the earth. Try to find one rich or famous person from the eighteenth century who's still around today. You won't be able to. They are all gone.

But I am still here. And my words in the Bible are still here. They are still as powerful as they have been from the beginning. My words will last through all time. They will outlast fame and money and weak human beings. So read the words of the Bible. They will live forever. And they will show you how to live forever with Jesus too.

The Everlasting,

God

=== ==========

DON'T BE AFRAID

But now, this is what the Lord says . . .
"Fear not, for I have redeemed you; I have
summoned you by name; you are mine."

| | | | Isaiah | | 43:1 | | | | | |

Dear Child,

>I want to tell you about one of your worst enemies. This enemy is not a person or an animal or a creature from space. It is an emotion. The enemy I'm talking about is fear.

Fear can tie you up in knots and paralyze you. It can keep you from being your best. It can keep you from living a happy life. I want you to treat fear just like you would treat any other enemy. Guard against it. Don't give it any space in your life.

I am a God of love, and there is no fear in love. I have great plans for you, and there is no room for fear in my plans. The more you trust me, the less time you will spend on being afraid.

The One Who Gives You Courage,

God

=== =========

E-mail from God for Kids

*The name of the Lord is a strong tower;
the righteous run to it and are safe.*

Proverbs	18:10

Dear Child,

>Back in the Middle Ages, people built huge castles with strong walls to protect themselves against their enemies. No matter what strong enemy was after them, they could always run to their castle and be safe. I want to be the strong castle in your life.

It doesn't matter if everything you do seems to fail. It doesn't matter if everyone seems to be against you. You can always run to me and be safe. Just call on the name of Jesus, and I'll lower the drawbridge for you. You can come in, and I will close the gates behind you, protect you, and help you figure out the best way to deal with what's going on in your life.

Run to me,

God

=== =========

THE ONE AND ONLY

For this is what the Lord says--
he who created the heavens, ...
"I am the Lord, and there is no other."

| Isaiah | 45:18 |

Dear Child of Mine,

>You might hear some people say that there are many roads to heaven, and any road will get you there as long as you really believe. Listen. You can really believe something and be really wrong. You can believe that the ocean is full of orange juice instead of salt water, but that won't change what's in the ocean. You can believe that the moon is made of cream cheese instead of rocks and dust, but that won't change what the moon is made of. You can believe that one god is as good as another, but that won't make it true.

I am the one and only true God. So don't waste your belief on imitations. Put your faith in me.

The One and Only,

God

=== =========

E-mail from God for Kids

SHOW-AND-TELL

This is how much God loved the world: He gave his Son, his one and only Son. And this is why: so that no one need be destroyed; by believing in him, anyone can have a whole and lasting life.

John 3:16 — THE MESSAGE

My Child,

>Do you remember show-and-tell in school, where everyone brought something to show the class? Well, imagine you had a puppy at home, and for show-and-tell, you wrote a long, very good speech about your puppy. Do you think your classmates would care? Probably not. But if you took that puppy to school, you wouldn't have to say anything but "This is my puppy." Your friends would think it was the best speech ever because they could see the puppy, touch it, and really know it.

For years I tried to tell men and women about my love for them. I spoke through prophets who gave awesome speeches and performed miraculous signs. But most of the people still didn't believe. So instead of just talking about it, I sent my love to earth in Jesus Christ to show people what love really is. Once you see Jesus and really know him, then you will understand my love for you.

The One Who Shows You Love,

God

=== =========

EYE OF THE HURRICANE

Jesus himself stood among them and said to them, "Peace be with you."

| Luke | 24:36 |

My child,

>Have you ever been in a hurricane? A hurricane is a powerful, swirling storm that can uproot trees and blow houses away. But there is a quiet place in the center of a hurricane's circular winds that is called the eye of the storm. In the eye of a hurricane, everything is still and quiet.

Sometimes life can feel like a hurricane. It gets busy and wild. There is too much to do and too many things to worry about. When that happens, Jesus can be the eye in the middle of your storm. He can come into all the hurry and the worry of your life and speak words of peace. He can make sense out of confusion and bring good things out of bad.

Trust my Son in the storms of life,

God

=== =========

E-mail from God for Kids

SHARE THE NEWS!

The first thing Andrew did was to find his brother Simon and tell him, "We have found the Messiah" (that is, the Christ). And he brought him to Jesus.

John 1:41–42

Dear Child,

>When you find a really good thing, don't you want to tell someone about it? Suppose you found a great new hamburger place that made awesome burgers. You probably wouldn't keep it a secret. You'd tell all your friends, wouldn't you?

When Andrew met Jesus, he knew he had found something better than a good hamburger. He had found the Son of God. So Andrew didn't waste time. He told his brother Simon. Then he took Simon to meet Jesus.

Have you met Jesus? Have you found out how awesome and powerful he is? If you have, do what Andrew did. Find someone who needs to know him and share the news!

The father of Jesus,

God

=== =========

THE CHOICE IS YOURS

Do not let your hearts be troubled.
Trust in God; trust also in me.

| John | 14:1 |

My child,

>Suppose one of your friends said something really mean about you. Would you suddenly become furious? You might even say that person made you mad. Well, let me tell you a secret. People cannot *make* you feel anything unless you let them. If you get angry or sad or hurt, it's because you chose to feel that way. You see, it's not what happens to you in life that's important. It's how you choose to react to what happens that really matters.

Jesus is telling you not to waste a lot of time being troubled and upset. Choose to trust him instead. No matter what happens to you today, trusting Jesus is the best choice to make. Because if you do, you will be choosing happiness.

Your father and friend,

God

=== =========

E-mail from God for Kids

GIVE THE GIFT AWAY

*Dear friends, since God so loved us,
we also ought to love one another.*

| 1 John | 4:11 |

Dear Child,

>I love giving you gifts. I do it all the time. The very best gift I give you is my love. But love is not a gift that you fold up and put in your bottom drawer where you never see it or use it. Love is a gift that is meant to be given away.

That's because love is the gift that everyone needs. Poor people need it. Rich people need it. People need it when they're winning and when they're losing. Smart people need it, and not-so-smart people need it. Kids need it. Teachers need it. Parents need it. The janitor in your school needs it. The president of the United States needs it. Your favorite movie star needs it. The lady working at McDonald's needs it. Nobody ever outgrows the need for love. Will you love someone for me today?

The Lord Who Loves You,

God

=== =========

SECRET TREASURE

*call to me and I will answer you and tell you
great and unsearchable things you do not know.*

| Jeremiah | 33:3 |

My child,

>When you find me, it's like you stumbled on a treasure chest full of the most amazing riches. I'm not just talking about money. I'm talking about salvation and a new life. When you see these first and most important gifts, it can seem like you've seen it all. But my riches don't just end there.

As you continue to walk with me, it's as if you keep finding secret drawers and doors in my treasure chest. These secret compartments just keep opening to show you new and wonderful things: adventures, challenges, victories, friendships, spiritual gifts, and lasting joy.

My gifts in your life never end. I never run out of things I want to show you and explain to you. But you have to keep searching out my treasure. If you do, you will have a life filled with great and wonderful riches.

Your Treasure,

God

=== =========

E-mail from God for Kids

ANOTHER KIND OF THIRST

Jesus answered, "Everyone who drinks this water will be thirsty again, but whoever drinks the water I give him will never thirst. Indeed, the water I give him will become in him a spring of water welling up to eternal life."

| John | 4:13-14 |

My child,

>After a long, hot day at the beach, nothing satisfies your physical thirst like a glass of cool water.   But you have another kind of thirst. It's called spiritual thirst.

It's hard to describe the feeling of spiritual thirst. It feels a little bit like being lonely or homesick—like missing the people you love when they are far away from you.

Jesus is the living water that satisfies this spiritual thirst. If you let him, he will pour that water into your life. He'll be the answer to your questions and take away your sad, lonely feelings. He'll stay by you when you're sad and encourage you when you need help. He's not bottled water or faucet water. He's living water, and that means he'll never dry up. He will always be there to satisfy your spiritual thirst.

The Father of Jesus,

God
=== ==========

WHO ARE YOU?

The Spirit himself testifies with our spirit that we are God's children.

| Romans | | 8:16 | |

Dear Child,

>If someone asked you who you are, what would you answer? Would you say, "I'm a sixth grader" or "I'm a pitcher on our baseball team" or "I'm the youngest of three sisters"? The way you describe yourself tells what you think of yourself.

Believe me, you are much more than a sixth grader or a pitcher or somebody's sister. My Holy Spirit is constantly whispering to your spirit, reminding you of who you are. You are my child, created uniquely and loved completely. You have a destiny—a personal map drawn for your life alone. You have a purpose—a reason for living, a hope for the future. You have a place—you are a child in the family of God.

Your Creator and Friend,

God

=== =========

E-mail from God for Kids

Jesus came and touched them.
"Get up," he said. "Don't Be Afraid."

| Matthew | 17:7 |

My Child,

>If you sit around all day thinking about things you're scared of, you're going to live a very fearful life. I don't want you to live like that. I want to make you strong enough to stand for me without fear, even in scary situations.

I'm not telling you to throw away your common sense and do something dumb just to prove how brave you are. But I am telling you this: I'm more powerful than anything you're scared of. I am in control, and I'm always with you.

Jesus spoke the words "Don't be afraid" many times to his friends. But he also touched them and stood by them in the scary times. That's what I want for you, too, my child.

So trust me and don't be afraid.

Your Protector,

God

=== =========

WORDS ARE CHEAP

The Lord says: "These people come near to me with their mouth and honor me with their lips, but their hearts are far from me."

| Isaiah | 29:13 |

Dear Child of Mine,

>Lots of people talk about me. They act as if they know me when they don't. What their mouths say and what their hearts believe are miles apart. Words are cheap. I'm more interested in what you believe in your heart than what you say with your mouth.

Have you ever sat in church, singing all the words of the songs without thinking about what they mean? Have you ever given the "right" answer in Sunday school even though you didn't really believe what you were saying? I don't want meaningless words sung about me. And I don't want heartless right answers. I just want you, my child. I want your love, your faith, and your whole heart.

Lord of the Heart,

God

=== =========

E-mail from God for Kids

I FINISH WHAT I START

He who began a good work in you will carry it
on to completion until the day of Christ Jesus.

| | Philippians | 1:6 | |

Dear Child,

>Suppose your dad promised to build you a cool tree fort
in your favorite tree. Suppose he bought all the wood and
the tools he would need and spent two days working
really hard on the tree fort. But on the third day, he put
the tools away and quit. Wouldn't you be disappointed?

I am the kind of Person who finishes what he starts. I
have started to build good things in your life. I have
started to build the kind of faith that will keep you strong.
I have begun to unfold gifts in you that I have plans to
use. Whatever it takes to make you completely mine,
that's what I will do. And nothing will stop me until the
job is done.

Your faithful Father,

God

=== =========

SELF-CONFIDENCE BEGINS WITH GOD-CONFIDENCE

Do not throw away your confidence;
it will be richly rewarded.

Hebrews | 10:35

My child,

>People are always telling you to develop self-confidence.
Here's my advice on that subject. The best way to
develop confidence in yourself is to put your confidence
in me.

Because you know that I am the God who made you and
will never let you down, you can really believe that you
are loved. Because I have unlimited strength and total
control, you can feel strong. Because I'm on your side,
you can believe that you won't be left hanging.

The more you know me, the more confidence you will
have in me and my strength. And the more confidence
you have in me and my strength, the more confidence you
will have in who you are. God-confidence always leads to
godly self-confidence. This is the kind of solid confidence
I want to give you.

The Source of Your Confidence,

God

=== =========

E-mail from God for Kids

Many are the plans in a man's heart,
but it is the Lord's purpose that prevails.

	Proverbs	19:21	

My child,

>"Aladdin and the Magic Lantern" is a story about a boy who found a magic lamp. All he had to do was rub the lamp, and a huge genie would pop out and give Aladdin whatever he asked for.

Don't get me mixed up with Aladdin's genie. I'm not here to grant every wish you make. You see, I know what will be good for you and what will be harmful. So sometimes I have to answer your prayers by saying "no."

Instead of asking me to bless your plans, why not ask me to show you my plans? Then we can work together. My plans may not be what you had in mind, but they will always bring the best things into your life.

The Lord of the Better Plan,

God

=== =========

THINK BEFORE YOU SPEAK

Consider what a great forest is set on fire by a small spark. The tongue also is a fire.

| | **James** | **3:5-6** | |

My Child,

>Smokey the Bear is the cartoon character that reminds campers to be careful with fire. He warns hikers never to drop a match in the forest, especially during dry weather. One little spark, and the whole forest could go up in flames.

People who are careless with words can cause as much damage as people who are careless with fire. Just throwing out a few thoughtless words of gossip can cause someone's feelings to "go up in flames." The hearts of my children need as much protection as the trees in my forests do. I don't want you to hurt them. So be very careful with your words, my child. Always think before you speak.

The One Who Hears and Cares,

God
=== =========

E-mail from God for Kids

DON'T WORRY ABOUT TOMORROW

Which of you by worrying can add a single hour to his life? Since you cannot do this very little thing, why do you worry about the rest?

| Luke | 12:25-26 |

My Child,

>There is one day in each week that should be kept free from worry and anxiety. That day is tomorrow. Do you ever spend time worrying about things that might happen in the future? Do you ever go to sleep at night dreading the next day?

Tomorrow is full of huge possibilities—possible victories, possible failures, possible highs and lows. But today, all of those things are out of your reach. Trying to control tomorrow is worrying about something that may never happen.

You can do your best today to study for a test or train for a race that will take place tomorrow. But beyond that, there's nothing you can do. So instead of spending your energy worrying and trying to guess what might happen tomorrow, spend that energy doing things today. Don't let tomorrow's overwhelming possibilities crowd out today's joys. Let me be in charge of tomorrow. Trust me, and spend your energy making today the best it can be.

Ruler of Tomorrow,

God

=== =========

CHOOSE ME!

If God is for us, who can be against us?

| Romans | 8:31 |

Dear Child of Mine,

>Suppose it was your job to choose the players for your team. Wouldn't you choose the strongest, smartest, quickest, most athletic players? Suppose you could choose me? Wouldn't you do it?

I am the most powerful being on any planet in the whole galaxy. (In fact, I created the galaxy!) I can outrun, outsmart, and outplay anyone on any team. Think about it. If I am on your side, it doesn't really matter who is on the other side. You're going to come out ahead.

Well, your life is more important than a game. I'm on your side as you live your life. So it doesn't matter who is against you. You are a winner!

The Key Player,

God
=== ==========

E-mail from God for Kids

YOUR DAD IS THE KING

For you did not receive a spirit that makes you a slave again to fear, but you received the Spirit of sonship. And by him we cry, "Abba, father."

Romans   **8:15**

My Child,

>If you were the child of a king, you could walk around your father's kingdom feeling pretty confident. Nobody would mess with the king's kid.

Well, I want you to live your everyday life just like the child of a king. Why? Because that's exactly who you are. I'm the King of everything in Heaven and earth, and I'm your Dad. That means wherever you go and whatever you face, I'll be there encouraging and protecting you. And because you're my child, everything in my kingdom will be yours. All the beauty, the music, the fun, the excitement, and the happiness. My time will be your time; my wisdom will be your wisdom; my family will be your family.

Celebrate who you are today—the beloved child of a powerful King.

Your Dad,

God

=== =========

YOU ARE THE KEY

We are God's workmanship, created in Christ Jesus to do good works, which God prepared in advance for us to do.

Ephesians　　**2:10**

Dear Child,

>Picture a whole box full of door keys. They might look very much alike, but each one has been cut to open a particular door. If you try to open the right door with the wrong key, it won't work.

You are like one of those keys. I designed you to do special things that no one else can do. There are special "doors" that I want you to open. There are special jobs that I want you to do for my kingdom. You are not just an accident that happened one day. Long before you were born, I knew exactly how I wanted to use your life. Give me your life, my child. Nothing in the world will make you happier.

The Key Maker,

God

=== =========

E-mail from God for Kids

MORE THAN YOU ASK OR IMAGINE

[God] is able to do immeasurably more than all we ask or imagine, according to his power that is at work within us.

.Ephesians | 3:20

Dear Child,

>Have you ever wanted something so badly for your birthday that you thought you'd die if you didn't get it? Then when you got it, you were tired of it in just a few weeks. Do you know why that happened? It's because sometimes you don't know what you really want and need.

But I know. Since I made you, I'm able to give you exactly what you want and need. I know what will be good for you. In fact, I can do better things for you than you could even dream up to ask me for. So don't be afraid to pray, "Father, I don't know what to ask for. So give me what you know will be good for me." I love to answer a prayer like that.

The Giver,

God

=== =========

LIKE MONEY IN THE BANK

*You need to persevere so that when
you have done the will of God, you
will receive what he has promised.*

Hebrews 10:36

Dear Child of Mine,

>My promises to you are your inheritance. They are like money in the bank under your name. But how do you get those promises out of the bank and into your life?

First, find out what I've put into your account. To do that, read the words of the promises on the pages of the Bible. (For instance, Luke 1:37 says, "Nothing is impossible with God.")

Next, write a check. To do that, believe what you read. (Choose to believe Luke 1:37: "Nothing is impossible with God.")

And finally, spend the promises. To do that, take action. (Trust me to help you accomplish something that once seemed impossible to you.)

Discover the excitement of trusting in my promises.

The Promise Keeper,

God
=== =========

E-mail from God for Kids

In the morning, O Lord, you hear my voice;
in the morning I lay my requests before
you and wait in expectation.

| | **Psalm** | **5:3** | | |

Dear Child,

>What's the most important thing you can do in the
morning? It's not eating breakfast or brushing your teeth
or combing your hair. The most important thing you can
do is to spend time with me.

Before you even push back the covers and put your foot
on the floor, think of me. Talk to me. Say, "Good
morning, God." Let me know you love me. Tell me what
you need. Do you want to make a good grade on your
test? Would you like to make a new friend? Are you
having trouble getting along with your sister or brother? I
care about whatever you care about. Talk to me first thing
in the morning and let me make your day a great one.

Your father and friend,

God

=== =========

TO TRUST IS TO LEAN ON ME

The Lord's unfailing love surrounds the man who trusts in him.

Psalm 32:10

My Dear Child,

>When a person has trouble walking, he sometimes leans on a crutch. The crutch helps him keep his balance so he can walk and not fall.

In a way, my love can be like a crutch for you. It will always be right beside you so you can lean on it and walk straight and steady. Leaning on my love, you can get through things that used to make you stumble. You'll be able to live a clean, strong life that I will be proud of. So trust me. I'll be with you every day, no matter what you're walking through. Lean on my love, and I won't let you fall.

The Lord of Unfailing Love,

God

=== =========

E-mail from God for Kids

Many are saying of me, "God will not deliver him."
... But you are a shield around me, O Lord.

| | Psalm | 3:2-3 | |

My Child,

>You might hear some kids saying that I'm not real. Some of them might say that you're dumb to believe in me because I can't help you. But I want you to know me so well that those kids don't even bother you.

So here's what to do. If you hear that kind of talk, pray silently to me. Say, "Father, I know you're real, and I know you can help me. Protect me like a shield so their words don't hurt me. Help me not to be mad at the kids who don't know you. Show me how to pray for them." When you ask me for these things, I will hear you and answer your prayer.

Your Shield,

God

=== =========

SHOW ME SOME ACTION

Dear Children, let us not love with words or tongue but with actions and in truth.

| 1 John | 3:18 |

Dear Child,

>What kind of person do you respect the most? The person who talks about giving money to the poor or the person who actually gives the money? The person who talks about helping people in need or the person who actually helps needy people?

I'm much more impressed by people who back up their words with action. A lot of talk never helped anyone. Listen. You could get up in the pulpit of the world's biggest church and preach a great sermon on love, but if you didn't love other people, I wouldn't be impressed by your sermon. So show me more than words. Show me some action!

Your Loving Father,

God

=== =========

E-mail from God for Kids

TELL SOMEONE TODAY

We have heard with our ears, O God; our fathers
have told us what you did in their days.

Psalm 44:1

Dear Child,

>You don't need to memorize the Bible or sing in the
choir or teach Sunday school to make my kingdom grow.
Those are good things to do, but the best way to spread
your faith is to tell the people around you every day about
the good things I am doing in your life.

Have I answered a prayer for you? Don't keep it to
yourself. Tell someone. Have I mended a friendship that
was broken? Let someone know. Have I helped you
make the right decision about something? Tell a friend all
about it. Share the small miracles I am working in your
life. My kingdom always grows when my people spread
the good news of who I am.

Tell someone today,

God

=== =========

MORE THAN AN ORDINARY FRIEND

In fear and amazement they asked one another, "Who is this? He commands even the winds and the water, and they obey him."

Luke	8:25

Dear Child,

>Jesus acted pretty normal most of the time. That's why his friends would sometimes think of him as "just one of the guys." But every once in a while he would do something so miraculous that it would shake them up.

That's what happened one day when they were out in a small boat and a huge storm came up. His friends were terrified, but Jesus calmly told the storm to quiet down. And it did!

Jesus wants to be your best friend, the friend you can talk to about everything. But never forget—he's much more than an ordinary friend. He's my Son. He's able to do powerful and wonderful things in your life. Trust him, and he will.

His Father and Yours,

God

=== =========

E-mail from God for Kids

LET YOUR FAITH SHINE

Neither do people light a lamp and put it under a bowl. Instead they put it on its stand, and it gives light to everyone in the house. In the same way, let your light shine before men, that they may see your good deeds and praise your father in heaven.

| Matthew | 5:15-16 |

My Child,

>It would be pretty dumb to turn on a lamp at night and then put a bucket over the lamp. The bucket would block out the light, and you'd still be in the dark.

When I live in your heart, I light up your life with my love. I want to shine in you so the people you know will see me in your life. Then some of them will want to get to know me like you do.

So learn to let your faith shine. You don't have to show off and act super holy about it. Just be yourself. Be the person I love. Care about others. And soon the light in you will begin to shine in their hearts too.

The Lamplighter,

God

=== =========

HAVE A JESUS ATTITUDE

Your attitude should be the same as that of Christ Jesus: Who . . . made himself nothing, taking the very nature of a servant, being made in human likeness.

  Philippians 2:5-7

Dear Child,

>Jesus could have shown up on earth one day with a shiny crown on his head, saying, "Everybody bow down; the King of Heaven has arrived!" But he wasn't like that. He came as a small, weak baby. He grew up as an ordinary boy in an ordinary town. He worked in his family's carpentry shop. Later, when he left home, he walked around the countryside teaching ordinary men and women about my love and my kingdom. Jesus wasn't stuck-up, even though he had every right to be. He was humble.

I want you to be like Jesus. Don't act like a big shot. Be humble and care about other people. The more you live like Jesus, the more you'll honor me.

The Lord of the Humble Heart,

God

=== =========

E-mail from God for Kids

IT'S SIMPLE, NOT EASY

But these are written that you may believe that Jesus is the Christ, the Son of God, and that by believing you may have life in his name.

John	20:31

My child,

>Becoming a Christian is not hard. Anyone of any age can do it. Do you believe that Jesus is my Son who came to earth to forgive people? Do you want to be forgiven? If you answered yes, then you can be a Christian.

Although becoming a Christian is simple, living like a Christian can be hard. It's hard to stand up for what's right when everyone else is doing what's wrong. It's hard to be nice to people who don't treat you with respect. It's hard to be my child in places where people don't believe in me or live by my words.

But here's the good news. When you make the simple decision to become a Christian, I will be with you, and I will help you to live like a Christian as well.

Your father and friend,

God

=== =========

I CAN MAKE THINGS NEW

He who was seated on the throne said,
"I am making everything new!"

  Revelation   **21:5**

My Child,

>Have you ever felt like you've messed something up so badly that there's no fixing it? Maybe it's a friend you've let down, a test that you've failed, or an athletic event where you've totally blown it.

No matter how bad you think things are, there's something I want you to know. You'll never totally blow it with me. I will never say to you, "Well, that's it. You've done it now. You and I are finished." You see, I am the God who has the power to make things new. I can breathe new life into every kind of failure, no matter how large or small. All you have to do is confess anything you've done wrong, and I'll forgive you. Then you can start over. So bring your failures to me, and I'll help you begin again.

The Lord of New Beginnings,

God

=== =========

E-mail from God for Kids

NOTHING CAN BLOW IT OUT

For I am convinced that neither death nor life, neither angels nor demons, neither the present nor the future, nor any powers, neither height nor depth, nor anything else in all creation, will be able to separate us from the love of God that is in Christ Jesus our Lord.

| | Romans | 8:38-39 | |

My Child,

>Did you ever have one of those trick birthday candles on your cake that just kept on burning? No matter how hard you blew on it, that little flame just kept popping up.

Well, my love for you is like that candle, only it's much more powerful. There's no way that anything can blow it out. My love is the one thing in your life that will last forever. There's no power in Heaven or on earth that can convince my heart to stop loving you. Time will go by, styles will change, countries will rise and fall, storms will rage, winds will blow. Your life on earth will even come to an end. But the flame of my love will still be burning. It will light your way to Heaven.

The Love That's Here to Stay,

God

=== =========

COME AWAY WITH ME

Very early in the morning, while it was still dark, Jesus got up, left the house and went off to a solitary place, where he prayed.

Mark 1:35

My child,

>Have you ever tried to talk to a close friend about something important while the television was blaring and people were walking in and out of the room? It's hard to have a conversation in the middle of so much confusion and noise. If you want to talk to your friend, it's better to go somewhere that's quiet. Then you'll be able to listen and hear.

I am your closest friend. I want to say important things to you. I want to help you make decisions. I want to tell you about the work I have for you to do. But if you are always surrounded by people and noise, you'll never hear my words. So, do what Jesus did. Go to a quiet place and listen.

The Friend Who Waits to Talk to You,

God

E-mail From God For Kids

GET THE HOOK UP

Both riches and honor come from You, and You rule over all, and in Your hand is power and might; and it lies in Your hand to make great and to strengthen everyone.

| 1 Chronicles | 29:12 NASB |

My Child,

>You could have a house with electrical wiring and a bunch of fancy electric appliances, but if that house isn't hooked up to the electric company, it will all be just for show.

In the same way, if you have everything going for you—looks, grades, skills, popularity—but you don't even know the one who gave you all of those things, then it's all just for your own pride. I have wired you a certain way, and that way includes being connected to me, the power source. Once you find me and know me, you'll start to see and understand things about yourself that may have been there all along. They just weren't lit up.

So hook up to me. Let me light up your life with my purpose, my strength, and my love.

The Power,

God

=== ========

BE REAL WITH ME

The sacrifices of God are a broken spirit; a broken and contrite heart, O God, you will not despise.

| Psalm | 51:17 |

My Child,

Is there one person in your life you can be 100 percent honest with? Maybe it's your mom or your youth pastor or a friend you trust. With that person, you don't have to pretend you're happy when you're not.

I'm longing for the day when you'll let me be that kind of friend to you. I don't want you to put on a happy face on the outside when you have a broken heart on the inside. I want to see your true feelings because they matter to me. I want you to be real with me. Let me be the one who dries your tears and heals your heartaches. Let me be the one you trust.

Your Healer and Friend,

God

=== =========

E-mail from God for Kids

SMALL THINGS MAKE A HUGE DIFFERENCE

If I have the gift of prophecy and can fathom all mysteries and all knowledge, and if I have a faith that can move mountains, but have not love, I am nothing.

| 1 Corinthians | 13:2 |

Dear Child,

>A very wise woman named Mother Teresa once said, "We cannot do great things in this world. We can only do small things with great love."

If there are times when you feel that you're not doing big, important things for me, don't sweat it. I don't need huge things from you. Instead, I want you to have a humble, loving heart. I want you to go through each day willing to do the small, loving things that will make a difference in the lives of other people.

Is there a kid in your class who needs help with his homework? Volunteer to help him. Does your mom seem frustrated and overworked? Help her out in the kitchen tonight. Small things done with love make a huge difference.

Lord of the Loving Heart,

God

=== =========

DON'T GIVE UP!

See! The winter is past; the rains are over and gone. Flowers appear on the earth; the season of singing has come.... The blossoming vines spread their fragrance.... Come with me.

 Song of Songs   2:11-13

My Child,

>It's easy to recognize the seasons of the earth. In winter everything seems dead and gone for good. Leaves fall off the trees. Flowers die. Daylight hours grow shorter. But in time, things begin to come to life again. Green buds appear on branches. Flowers begin to poke through the soil. And soon springtime takes over again.

Your heart goes through seasons too. When you're sad, it can feel like winter in your heart. It can feel like your hope is dying. But don't give up! I promise you, spring is never very far away. Let me lead you through the winter of your heart into a new season of hope and happiness.

The Lord of All Seasons,

God

=== =========

E-mail from God for kids

LOOK UP!

*I lift up my eyes to you, to you
whose throne is in heaven.*

| Psalm | 123:1 |

Dear Child,

>Every day of your life you have a choice. You can walk around hanging your head, looking at the ground, feeling bad about life. Or you can look up. You can look at the trees, the sky, and the clouds. You can remember who made all those beautiful things and feel good.

It's your choice. You can have a bad attitude and an ungrateful heart. Or you can have a good attitude and a grateful heart. You can think about what's not going right, and you can gripe about it. Or you can think about the good things in your life and thank me for them.

My advice to you is to look up, my child.

Look up to me,

God

=== =========

I'VE ALREADY GIVEN YOU THE BEST

He who did not spare his own Son, but gave him up for us all--how will he not also, along with him, graciously give us all things?

| Romans | 8:32 |

Dear Child of Mine,

>Am I a good God? You bet I am! Come on. Just think about it. Look at what I've already given you. I gave you a beautiful planet for your home. Sure, sometimes people pollute it and throw trash on it. But you've got to admit—my basic creation is outstanding.

I've given you free air to breathe and lungs that do their own breathing. You don't have to say, "Now I'll breathe. In, out, in, out." I just made you with an automatic "breather" that keeps you alive.

But best of all, I gave you my perfect Son to live and die for you so that you could have a friendship with me. I've already given you the best, my child. Don't you think you can trust me to give you everything else you need?

The Giver,

God

=== =========

E-mail from God for Kids

God is our refuge and strength, an ever-present help in trouble. Therefore we will not fear, though the earth give way and the mountains fall into the heart of the sea.

Psalm 46:1-2

Dear Child of Mine,

>Have you ever seen a movie about a terrible disaster? Maybe it was about a giant flood or a man-eating shark or an ape taller than a skyscraper. Sometimes a scary movie seems so real that you can imagine what that disaster would really be like. You can almost feel the fear taking over.

Well, I've got news for you. Even if the worst disaster came true, you would have nothing to fear. Even if the earth fell apart and the mountains crumbled, you would be safe in my care. I made the earth and the mountains and the floods. I made the sharks and the apes. I am in total control; so don't sweat it. I've got you covered.

Your Defender,

God

=== =========

BE A PEACEMAKER

Blessed are the peacemakers, for they will be called sons of God.

	Matthew	5:9	

Dear Child,

>The world can be a place filled with fussers and fighters. Countries declare war over little differences. Friends break off their friendships over the smallest things. That's because a lot of people think that being right is more important than being at peace. You can spend your whole life trying to be right, and you won't have a moment's peace.

I want a better life for you. I want you to be a peacemaker. The more you know me, the more you'll understand how to bring love and peace into the middle of arguing and fighting. I will help you be humble enough to make my peace more important than your pride. When you become a peacemaker, you will truly be living as my child.

The Peace Lover,

God

=== =========

E-mail from God for Kids

As Jesus was walking beside the Sea of Galilee, he saw two brothers, Simon called Peter and his brother Andrew. . . . "Come, follow me," Jesus said, "and I will make you fishers of men." At once they left their nets and followed him.

| | Matthew | 4:18-20 | |

My child,

>Jesus asked lots of people to follow him. Some people didn't follow because they were too busy. Some didn't follow because they were afraid a life with Jesus would be hard or uncomfortable. Some people didn't follow because they didn't want to leave their familiar way of life.

But Andrew and Peter didn't waste time. The minute Jesus asked them to follow him, they did.

What about you? Have you heard my Son's invitation? Are you too busy with friends or schoolwork to follow? Are you afraid that following Jesus will be too hard? Are you too attached to your life the way it is? I promise you this: There is no adventure in the world like following Jesus. Andrew and Peter found that out. You can too. Follow my Son.

Lord of the Adventure,

God

=== =========

JOIN THE FAMILY

For whoever does the will of my Father in heaven is my brother and sister and mother.

| | | | | | Matthew | | 12:50 | | | | | |

Dear Child,

>Jesus has a huge family. He has sisters and brothers in different countries all across the world. These sisters and brothers may not look like him. Their skin may be black or white or red or yellow. Their eyes may be brown or hazel or blue or green. They may be tall or short, fat or thin. But they all have one thing in common. They have decided to trust Jesus as their Lord. They have decided to spend every day doing things his way.

Belonging to the family of Jesus is a guarantee that you will never be alone. My Son will live in your heart, my Spirit will guide you, and I will watch over you with my love. And you'll have the fun of meeting sisters and brothers everywhere you go.

The Father of the family,

God

=== =========

E-mail from God for Kids

JESUS IN DISGUISE

I tell you the truth, whatever you did for one of the least of these brothers of mine, you did for me.

| Matthew | 25:40 |

Dear Child,

>Would you be surprised if I told you that you could see Jesus every day? Well, you can! How is that possible? Jesus told his followers that if they were kind to lonely people, they were being kind to him. If they fed hungry people, they were feeding him. If they visited sick people, they were visiting him. If they invited someone with no friends into their homes, they were inviting him.

Jesus hurts for people who are hurting. He feels their hunger and their loneliness. So when you help one of those people, Jesus is right there with you. It's like everyone in need is really Jesus in disguise.

Your Loving Father,

God

=== =========

FOLLOW THIS FORMULA

In everything, do to others what you would have them do to you, for this sums up the Law and the Prophets.

Matthew	7:12

Dear Child,

>I hope by now you've decided to live for me. But maybe you're thinking, *How can God expect me to do everything he wants me to do? I don't know all of his rules. I don't know the Bible by heart.*

Listen. I don't expect you to memorize the whole Bible. Here's how to know you're doing things my way. Treat other people the way you want them to treat you. Would you like your friend to share his stuff with you? Then share your stuff with him. It's that simple. Just think, *How do I want other people to act toward me?* Then act that way toward other people. This is called the "Golden Rule," and it really works.

Try it. You'll see.

Lord of the "Golden Rule,"

God

=== ==========

E-mail from God for Kids

CHOOSE THE NARROW ROAD

Enter through the narrow gate. For wide is the gate and broad is the road that leads to destruction, and many enter through it. But small is the gate and narrow the road that leads to life, and only a few find it.

| Matthew | 7:13-14 |

My child,

>Suppose you saw two roads. One was wide and easy and crowded with people having fun. But at the end of the road was a big mud pit where people were falling in and staying stuck. The other road was narrow. It was harder to walk on and not as crowded. But at the end of it was a beautiful kingdom where Jesus waited with open arms.

If you had a choice, of course you'd choose the road with the good ending. But lots of people go down the mud-pit path because they can't see where it ends.

Living for me is the narrow road. It can be hard at times; but when you reach my kingdom, you'll know it was worth it.

Choose the narrow road,

God

=== =========

PUT ON A NEW LIFE

You're done with that old life. It's like a filthy set of ill-fitting clothes you've stripped off and put in the fire. Now you're dressed in a new wardrobe... God picked out for you: compassion, kindness, humility, quiet strength, discipline.

Colossians 3:9–12   THE MESSAGE

My Child,

>I want you to take off your old way of acting, almost like you'd take off a set of filthy old clothes. Take off your bad temper, your meanness, and your lying and put them into the fire.

Let me give you a new way of living. It will be like a new set of clothes to put on. Put on love and kindness and humbleness and strength. When you put on these new "clothes," you'll be dressing yourself like Jesus.

At first your new clothes might feel a little bit uncomfortable. You might even think they will never fit you just right. But just keep dressing your heart in these new Christlike attitudes, and, in time, they'll be a perfect fit.

These clothes were made for you!

God

=== =========

E-mail from God for Kids

I AM HERE—ALIVE AND REAL!

These people are blockheads! They stick their fingers in their ears so they won't have to listen; they screw their eyes shut so they won't have to look, so they won't have to deal with me face-to-face and let me heal them.

Acts 28:27 | THE MESSAGE

My Child,

>Sometimes I'm amazed at how stubborn some people can be. They make up their minds that there is no God, and they refuse even to look at the evidence that I am real. My presence in the world is so obvious that they practically have to plug up their ears so they won't hear the truth. They almost have to cover their eyes to keep from seeing what's right in front of them.

I am here—alive and real! I have been here all along. I am the one who created human beings in the first place. Don't be a blockhead and close your eyes and ears to what's right in front of you. Open your eyes to see me, and open your ears to hear my voice.

The Lord of Love,

God

=== =========

WHERE DO YOU FIT IN?

Let's see how inventive we can be in encouraging love and helping out, not avoiding worshipping together ... but spurring each other on.

Hebrews 10:24 | THE MESSAGE

Dear Child,

>I created you with a powerful imagination. You've got great ideas. So I'm giving you a job. See what kind of ideas you can come up with for encouraging other people and helping them out.

Look around. There are people all around you who need help and encouragement. There are working moms who need after-school childcare. There are kids with learning problems who could use tutoring. There are children from broken homes who could use a kid like you as a friend. There are kids whose parents never take them to church who might love to go with you and your family.

Where do you fit into these problems? How can you help?

The Problem Solver,

God

=== =========

E-mail from God for Kids

WORRYING IS NO WAY TO LIVE

Don't . . . worry. Instead of worrying, pray. . . .
Shape your worries into prayers, letting God know
your concerns. Before you know it, a sense of God's
wholeness . . . will come and settle you down.

Philippians 4:6–7 | THE MESSAGE

My Child,

>How much time do you spend worrying about stuff like,
"What if it rains the day of the big game?" Or, "What if I
don't get asked to the party?" Or, "What if I don't make a
passing grade in math class?"

Worrying is no way to live. It's a waste of time because it
doesn't change a thing. Can worrying stop the rain or
guarantee you a passing grade in math? Of course not!
So instead of worrying about things, start praying about
them. Shape your worries into prayers and give them to
me.

Your Security,

God

P.S. By the way, as you're praying for your math test,
don't forget to study for it as well. That's doing your part.

=== ==========

JESUS IS THE GOAL

friends, don't get me wrong: By no means do I count myself an expert in all of this, but I've got my eye on the goal, where God is beckoning us onward to Jesus. I'm off and running and I'm not turning back.

Philippians 3:13-14   THE MESSAGE

Dear Child,

>You've probably never seen an Olympic runner line up on the track for his race and then suddenly jump out of his lane and run off the track, out of the stadium, and down the street. Any practiced runner knows that he's got to stay in his lane and keep his eye on the finish line if he expects to win a medal.

Your life is like a race, and I want you to keep your goal in mind. My Son, Jesus, is your goal. Every day, move closer to him. In every situation, try to be more like him. Being fast isn't good enough. You have to stay focused in your lane and run this race for all you're worth.

Your coach and your fan,

God

=== =========

E-mail from God for Kids

YOU HAVE A FRIEND

This is the very best way to love.
Put your life on the line for your friends.

| | John 15:13 | THE MESSAGE | | |

My Child,

>Suppose you and your best friend were crossing a busy city street. Suddenly you saw a truck ignoring the stoplight and heading right toward the two of you. Would you run for your life or risk your life? Would you try to save yourself or try to save your friend?

Lots of people would run for their own lives. But a few might think first of the safety of a friend. Jesus is your friend. Jesus had the power to escape the cross and save his own life. But that's not what he did. He went through the pain of dying on the cross to save you.

What did he save you from? Everlasting death. What did he save you for? Everlasting life with me. What a friend you have in Jesus!

His Father and Yours,

God
=== =========

LET YOUR FAITH SHAPE YOUR LIFE

Don't become so well-adjusted to your culture that you fit into it without even thinking. Instead, fix your attention on God. You'll be changed from the inside out.

Romans 12:2 **THE MESSAGE**

My Child,

>Suppose the police were arresting everyone who acted like Jesus. Would you be in danger of being arrested? Or would the police look at your life and say, "Nope. This one's nothing like Jesus. This one's just like all those other kids who don't believe in God"?

Here's the point I'm making. I don't want you to become so much like everyone around you that no one can even tell you're a Christian. What you believe on the inside should affect how you act on the outside. Think about your choices, your actions, and your behavior. Do they show your faith? Keep your mind and heart on me, and I'll begin to change you from the inside out.

The Life Transformer,

God

E-mail from God for Kids

MORE THAN QUARTERS AND DOLLARS

So here's what I want you to do, God helping you: Take your everyday, ordinary life—your sleeping, eating, going-to-[school], and walking-around life—and place it before God as an offering.

Romans 12:1 | THE MESSAGE

Dear Child,

>When you go to church, do you put money in the collection plate? That's a great thing to do, but you're old enough now to understand that I want more from you than quarters or dollars. What I really want is your whole life. No kidding! I mean it. Not just your Sunday school life but your whole life—your waking-and-sleeping, working-and-playing, laughing-and-crying life.

I know that seems like a lot to give, and it is. But think about it—you'll just be giving me something that I gave you in the first place. I designed you to be mine—to live in a loving Father-child relationship with me. Your life will never be all that it can be until you put it in my hands.

Your Loving Father,

God

=== =========

LOVE IS SERIOUS BUSINESS

Love from the center of who you are; don't fake it.

Romans 12:9	THE MESSAGE

My child,

>Have you ever been around someone who seemed very loving and sweet, but there was something about him or her that made you think the whole thing was just an act?

Listen. Love is serious business. It's the most important part of who you are and what you do. That's why I never want you to fake it. Let me live in your heart. I will make your love for other people real. It will bubble up from inside of you just like clear spring water bubbles up from the ground. Don't allow your love to be polluted by selfishness or jealousy.

If you ever feel like you're faking it, pray to me. Ask me to give you love that's real, and I will send my own love through you to others.

The Lord of Love,

God

=== =========

E-mail from God for Kids

Run for dear life from evil;
hold on for dear life to good.

Romans 12:9 | **THE MESSAGE**

My Child,

>Experimenting with evil is dangerous business. Some kids think they'll shoplift something small just for kicks, and no harm is done. But even if they never get caught, deep down where no one can see, that "harmless" thing hurts them.

Some kids believe they can use drugs and not be hurt by it. That's not true. Even if they never become addicted, they have hurt themselves by doing something they know is wrong.

Every choice is an important choice. So run from what you know is bad and hold on to what you know is good. Your life is precious to me.

Your Loving Dad,

God

=== =========

BE LIKE THE TORTOISE

Don't burn out; keep yourselves fueled and aflame. Be alert servants of the Master, cheerfully expectant. Don't quit in hard times; pray all the harder.

Romans 12:11–12   THE MESSAGE

Dear Child,

>Have you ever heard the story of the tortoise and the hare? The hare was the fastest rabbit around. He had the potential to win every race he ran. The tortoise was a slow-moving, clumsy, old turtle, but he had heart.

One day the hare challenged the tortoise to a race. The hare took off at full speed and passed the tortoise in no time. Then he got lazy and decided to take a nap. But the tortoise just kept plugging along, doing his very best. And in the end, the tortoise won the race.

I want you to have a heart like the tortoise's. Keep moving toward me. Stay excited. Keep your faith. Even in hard times, keep trusting and praying. You'll be the winner.

The Lord of the Race,

God

E-mail from God for Kids

SHARE YOUR HOME

Be inventive in hospitality.

Romans 12:13 | THE MESSAGE

My Child,

>If you live in a house, you're rich! (Lots of people live on the streets or under bridges.) If you've got your own room, you're blessed! (Lots of families live in one-room apartments where no one has a separate room.) If you have a family who loves you and believes in me, you've got the best gift of all.

Don't keep the blessings of your home to yourself. Share them with a friend. Make sure it's okay with your parents; then invite someone over. Pray about the person you want to invite. You might want to choose someone who doesn't have many friends. Think of ways to make your guest feel special. You can spread my love by sharing your home with others.

The Open Door,

God

=== ==========

I'LL LEND YOU MY EYES OF LOVE

Get along with each other; don't be stuck-up.
Make friends with nobodies;
don't be the great somebody.

Romans 12:16 | THE MESSAGE

Dear Child,

>I want you to love everyone—even people who get on your nerves, even the people you don't like very much.

I like everybody. I look at everybody through eyes of love. That's how I know each person is important. I want you to see people the way I see them. Let me lend you my eyes of love. Put them on like a pair of glasses, and you'll see clearly what I see: Everyone needs love and friendship. And everyone is worth it.

So don't be stuck-up. Treat everyone the same. Treat everyone with respect. They're all my children, and they deserve it.

Your Loving Father,

God

=== ==========

E-mail from God for Kids

FIGHT BAD WITH GOOD

Don't let evil get the best of you;
get the best of evil by doing good.

Romans 12:21   THE MESSAGE

My Child,

>You can't fight fire with fire. If you try it, you'll only end up with a bigger fire. To fight fire, you need water.

Just like you can't fight fire with fire, you can't fight bad stuff with more bad stuff. The best way to beat what's bad is by doing what's good.

Here's an example. Suppose some bullies at your school started picking on a kid who was really small for his age. You could start picking on the bullies and cause the whole thing to blow up into a huge fight. Or you could do something good. You could start treating the small kid with respect. Make friends with him. Stand up for him. Soon, the bullies will get tired of ragging on him. They might even learn to like him.

Stay on the good side,

God
=== =========

DON'T MISS THE ADVENTURE

The words I say to you are not just my own.
Rather, it is the Father, living in me,
who is doing his work.

| John | 14:10 |

Dear Child,

>Jesus was totally tuned in to me. He was fueled by my Spirit-power. He did what I wanted him to do. If he said something, you could be sure it was something I had told him to say.

He wasn't a puppet. He was a person who had a choice. But he always used that choice to live his life for me. That's why his life was so amazing.

Now, here's my message to you. It's your choice. You can choose to have an amazing life too. How? Let Jesus live in you. Let my Spirit-power be your fuel. Read the Bible and pray. Listen for my words in your heart and follow me.

Don't miss the adventure!

God
=== =========

E-mail from God for Kids

I'LL FILL YOUR WEAKNESS WITH MY STRENGTH

It was a case of Christ's strength moving in on my weakness. Now I take limitations in stride.... I just let Christ take over! And so the weaker I get, the stronger I become.

2 Corinthians 12:9-10   THE MESSAGE

My Child,

>If a muscle-bound weight lifter lifts five hundred pounds, people will be impressed with the weight lifter. But if a ninety-pound weakling asks me to help him lift five hundred pounds and he does it, people will be impressed with me.

If a great speaker makes a great speech, people will be impressed with the speaker. But if a shy person asks me to speak through her, people will be impressed with my speech.

Any time you let me fill your weakness with my strength, people will see me working in your life. So call on me when you feel scared or shy or weak, and I'll show up.

Your Strength and Power,

God

=== =========

AND THE WINNER IS . . .

The one who is in you is greater than the one who is in the world.

1 John	4:4

My Child,

>The devil acts tough and makes a lot of noise about how scary and powerful he is. But you don't need to go around feeling spooked by the devil. If you have invited Jesus to live in your heart, you've already got the devil beat.

It's a simple matter of what beats what. Just like a seven-point touchdown always beats a three-point field goal in football, the power of Jesus in you always beats the power of the devil in the world. Jesus defeated Satan on the cross. It's a plain fact. I know it. The devil knows it. And now you know it.

So don't waste another minute feeling afraid of the devil. Call on Jesus, and you've won the game!

The Father of Jesus,

God

=== =========

E-mail from God for Kids

But seek first his kingdom and his righteousness, and all these things will be given to you as well.

| | | Matthew | 6:33 | | |

Dear Child,

>If you made a list of all the stuff you needed, how long would your list be? One page? Two pages? Ten pages? The truth is, you don't really need all that much to be happy. Some of the things you think you need are really just things you want.

I'll tell you how to make a very short list of what you need. Start with a clean sheet of paper. Write a number one at the top, and beside it write "A relationship with God and his Son, Jesus." That would cover it. You see, I am all you really need because when I am in your life I give you everything else that's important. I give you what will make you truly happy.

Number One,

God
=== =========

LEARN FROM THE FARMERS

Remember this: Whoever sows sparingly will also reap sparingly, and whoever sows generously will also reap generously.

| | | 2 Corinthians | | 9:6 | | |

My child,

>Farmers know something that you should know. Whatever you plant is what you will harvest when your crop comes up. If you only plant a few seeds, you won't have much of a crop. But if you plant lots and lots of seeds, you'll have a huge harvest.

The same thing is true in your life. If you plant sarcasm and frowns and stinginess in your field of friendship, you won't grow many friends. But if you plant kind words and smiles and generosity in your friendship field, many friendships will begin to grow.

Learn the lesson of planting and harvesting, sowing and reaping. Put the very best you have into your life, and you will find that life will return to you the best it has to offer.

The Lord of the Harvest,

God

=== =========

E-mail from God for Kids

PRAISE BEFORE THE BATTLE

Jehoshaphat appointed men to sing to the Lord and to praise him ... as they went out at the head of the army.... As they began to sing and praise, the Lord set ambushes against the men ... who were invading Judah, and they were defeated.

2 Chronicles 20:21-22

My Child,

>When Judah was being attacked by foreign armies, King Jehoshaphat did something unusual. He appointed a big group of singers to march ahead of his soldiers, praising me.

In their songs, they were thanking me for my protection even before the battle. As their songs of praise reached my ears in Heaven, I was so pleased by their faith, I decided to defeat their enemies then and there. Judah never even had to fight! They just praised me, and I did the rest.

This is a good lesson for you to remember, my child. When you are worried about something in your life, start praising me for what I will do even before I do it. Trust me, and I'll be on your side.

Your Deliverer,

God

=== =========

A ROOM IS WAITING

In my father's house are many rooms; if it were not so, I would have told you. I am going there to prepare a place for you.

| | John | 14:2 | |

My Child,

>Is your room a special place for you? Is it painted your favorite color? Is it the place where you keep all of your favorite stuff—a place to take a friend who comes to visit?

If you don't have a room of your own, you'd probably like to have one. Well, I want you to know that there's a special room for you in my heavenly house. Jesus himself has gotten it ready just for you. It's a place where you can kick off your shoes and be at home.

Even though it's hard to explain Heaven in earthly words, I want you to be excited about the special place that's waiting for you. It's better than anything you could have dreamed up. You're going to love it!

The Home Owner,

God

=== =========

E-mail from God for Kids

GET OUT OF THE RAINSTORM

Thomas said to him, "Lord, we don't know where you are going, so how can we know the way?" Jesus answered, "I am the way and the truth and the life. No one comes to the father except through me."

John	14:5-6

My Child,

>Suppose you're trying to find a friend's house that you have never seen before. You're stumbling around in the dark in a rainstorm without a map.

Then all of a sudden you see the headlights of a car. The car slows down. The driver rolls down his window and calls your name. You realize it's your friend's father. Safe in the car of your friend's father, you know you're heading in the right direction.

Are you trying to get to me? Jesus is like the headlights that you see on a dark night. He's like a map that leads straight to me. There is no other way to reach me except through him. So get out of the rainstorm and into the car. Come home to me.

The One Who Waits for You,

God

=== =========

WHO WAS THIS GUY?

Philip said, "Lord, show us the Father and that will be enough for us." Jesus answered: "Don't you know me, Philip, even after I have been among you such a long time? Anyone who has seen me has seen the Father."

John 14:8-9

Dear Child,

>Philip and the other disciples were constantly trying to figure Jesus out. Who was this guy who came from a little town down the road but talked about his "home" in Heaven? Who was this guy who walked around in sandals doing amazing miracles?

It took the disciples a long time to understand that Jesus was just like me. He was God in human form. He was the walking, talking, breathing version of my love, my truth, my wisdom, and my way. That's why he said to Philip, "Anyone who has seen me has seen the Father."

Make no mistake about it, my child; if you know Jesus, you know me.

Like Father, Like Son,

God

=== =========

E-mail from God for kids

FIND YOUR FUN IN ME

Delight yourself in the Lord and he will give you the desires of your heart.

Psalm 37:4

Dear Child,

>Some people say that if you chase a butterfly, you'll never catch it. But sometimes if you stop chasing it, the butterfly will come and land right on your head.

Chasing happiness can be like that. If you chase happiness too hard, it will sometimes fly away and stay just out of your grasp.

I will tell you the key to catching true happiness. Stop chasing it. Find your fun in getting to know me and my people instead. And suddenly you'll look up one day and realize that you are filled with the happiness you've always wanted. Why? Because I made you to find your joy in me and to find your best friendships in my family.

The Key to True Happiness,

God

=== =========

WHAT'S THE CATCH?

I tell you the truth, anyone who has faith in me will do what I have been doing. He will do even greater things than these, because I am going to the Father.

| John | 14:12 |

Dear Child of Mine,

>Is Jesus "putting you on" when he says you'll be able to do greater things than he did? He was the faith-walking, mercy-talking, miracle-working Son of God, and the things he did were powerful.

He healed sick bodies, changed dishonest hearts, and set people free from their sins. He loved all the lonely, tired, unhappy men and women and children that he met. How is it possible for you to do things like that?

It's not possible on your own. But when you trust Jesus, my Holy Spirit works through you. He gives you my power to do amazing, Jesus-like things.

Believe it, my child,

God

=== =========

E-mail from God for Kids

FULL-TIME FRIEND

The Holy Spirit, whom the Father will send in my name, will teach you all things and will remind you of everything I have said to you.

| John | 14:26 |

Dear child,

>When you want to remember something, do you ever write yourself a note or tie a string around your finger?

I want you to know all day long that you belong to Jesus. So I've made it easy for you. I've given you a Friend to stay with you and remind you of all the powerful words Jesus has spoken. He's a Friend who never leaves you and always encourages you to be your best. He is my Holy Spirit.

My Spirit living in you shows you what Jesus wants you to do in every situation—at school, at home, with friends, or alone. Even though you can't see my Holy Spirit, he gives you the power you need to live like Jesus lived. Learn to listen to his silent voice inside.

The Spirit-giver,

God

=== =========

WHAT A GIFT!

Peace I leave with you; my peace I give you. I do not give to you as the world gives. Do not let your hearts be troubled and do not be afraid.

| John | 14:27 |

My child,

>Notice all the uptight people around you—gripping their steering wheels in traffic, looking nervously at their watches as they wait in line.

People try all kinds of things to get peace. Some try exercise. Some go shopping. Some try alcohol or drugs to stop the nervousness inside. But none of those things bring real peace.

Even in the midst of a nervous world, I can give you the gift of my peace that is real. My peace is something the world can't understand or imitate. It comes quietly into your heart when you put your trust in me.

The Peace-giver,

God
=== =========

E-mail from God for Kids

YOU'VE GOT A FRIEND

I no longer call you servants, because a servant does not know his master's business. Instead, I have called you friends, for everything that I learned from my father I have made known to you.

| John | | 15:15 | |

My Child,

>Suppose you had a secret that you wanted to tell another person. Whom would you tell? Would you tell some guy who works at a service station near your house, or would you tell your best friend? Duh. You'd tell your friend, right? Right!

The small group of people who followed Jesus had thought of him as their master and their teacher. But on the last night of his life, Jesus told those people that they were his friends. He told them his secrets and revealed my word and my plan to them.

Jesus wants to share his secrets with you too. He wants to unlock every mystery of his amazing love to you. He wants you to be his friend. Why not let him?

His Father,

God

=== ==========

YOU WERE ALWAYS ON MY MIND

You did not choose me, but I chose you.

| John | 15:16 |

Dear Child,

>Do you remember the first time you thought about getting to know me? Maybe it was when you were a little kid in Sunday school and you heard about my love for you. Maybe it was when somebody gave you this book. Reading these pages, maybe you suddenly said to yourself, "Hey, if God really loves me as much as he says, maybe I should find out more about him."

I want you to know that I loved you long before you first thought about loving me back. You were on my mind long before I even created you. You might think you chose me, but I was the one who chose you first. I have always wanted you to be my child.

The One Who Chose You,

God
=== =========

E-mail from God for Kids

If the world hates you, keep in mind that it hated me first.

| John | 15:18 |

Dear Child of Mine,

>When things don't work out like you hoped they would, when you try to do the right thing and people get the wrong idea, does it ever feel like the whole world is against you?

Jesus knew that feeling. When he was on earth, many people misunderstood him. Even though he always told the truth, some people called him a liar. Even though everything he did was good, some people decided he was bad. He was an innocent man who was found guilty. He deserved life, but he was put to death.

Living your life for Jesus won't always make you popular. But you will be in good company. Jesus wasn't always popular either.

His Father and Yours,

God
=== =========

THE QUICKEST WAY TO GOD'S HEART

The father himself loves you because you have loved me and have believed that I came from God.

| John | 16:27 |

My child,

>Suppose you got separated from your parents in a strange city and you were totally lost. If a kind policeman helped you find your way back to your parents, do you think they'd be grateful? You bet! They'd love that policeman. The quickest way to the heart of a parent is to be good to that parent's child.

I'm like that too. The quickest way to my heart is through my Son, Jesus. When you love Jesus, when you believe that he came from me, when you choose every day to live for him and follow in his footsteps, my heart fills up with love for you. So trust Jesus today and feel my love flow into your life.

His Grateful Parent,

God
=== ==========

E-mail from God for Kids

YOUR FAITH ADDS FLAVOR

You are the salt of the earth. But if the salt loses its saltiness, how can it be made salty again?

| Matthew | 5:13 |

Dear Child,

>Can you picture yourself eating potato chips made without any salt? They would taste bland and boring. Salt is one of the most popular seasonings in the world.

Jesus told his followers, "You are the salt of the world." He wanted to use their lives as seasoning for a bland world. He wanted their joy and enthusiasm to add flavor to the ordinary things of life.

Jesus wants you to be salt to the world you live in too. Kids at your school who don't know me have no idea how exciting a life of faith can be. They don't know what an adventure they're missing. Jesus wants to sprinkle you and your Christian friends like salt into this godless world. Don't lose your flavor.

Lord of the Adventure,

God

=== =========

I HAVE X-RAY VISION

*Your father knows what you need
before you ask him.*

| | | | | | Matthew | 6:8 | | | | |

Dear Child,

>I have a special kind of X-ray vision. My eyes of love can look inside your heart and see what you need even before you see it. There is nothing that makes me happier than meeting your needs and giving you what I know will bless you.

So don't feel like you have to make long lists of things you want me to do for you. Don't feel like you have to give me directions on how to help you. Trust me. I know what is best. When you pray, just ask me to guide you. Ask me to meet your needs my way. Someday you'll realize that, all along, my eyes could see what was best for you.

The Heart-reader,

God
=== =========

E-mail from God for Kids

GET GOOD AT FORGIVING

If you forgive men when they sin against you, your heavenly father will also forgive you. But if you do not forgive men their sins, your father will not forgive your sins.

| Matthew | 6:14-15 |

Dear Child,

>When you do something hateful or dishonest, how long does it take me to forgive you? No time at all. You only have to confess your sin, and I forgive you right away.

Now suppose your friend said something mean that hurt and embarrassed you. How long would it take you to forgive your friend? How many apologies would it take? How long would you hold on to your hurt feelings? How long would you refuse to forgive?

When you don't forgive someone else, it keeps you from being able to receive the forgiveness I have for you. That's why I want you to get good at forgiving others. Then my forgiveness for you can always reach you when you need it.

The Forgiver,

God

=== =========

MAKE ROOM FOR MY SON

And she gave birth to her firstborn, a son. She wrapped him in cloths and placed him in a manger, because there was no room for them in the inn.

| Luke | 2:7 |

Dear Child,

>Bethlehem was so busy and crowded the night Mary and Joseph came to town that there was no room for them at the inn. There was no room for the Son of God to be born.

Maybe if the people in Bethlehem had known who Jesus was, they would have made a place for the birth of my Son. But they didn't know.

Jesus is still looking for a welcoming place. He is looking for a man, a woman, or a young person who will make room for him in their lives. If you are too busy with school and friends and after-school activities, you will be like Bethlehem was that night. There will be no room for Jesus in your crowded life. But I hope you will make room in your heart so my Son can find a welcoming place in you.

His Father and Yours,

God

=== =========

E-mail from God for Kids

GOD'S GREATEST HEADLINE

But the angel said to them, "Do not be afraid. I bring you good news of great joy that will be for all the people. Today in the town of David a Savior has been born to you; he is Christ the Lord."

Luke 2:10-11

Dear Child,

>When you turn on the TV news, most of it is bad. There are plane crashes and floods and wars and violence. But back when the angel announced the Savior's birth, the news was totally good. In fact, it was amazing news, news of a great joy. And not for just a few people, but for all people—everyone, everywhere.

His birth meant hope for the hopeless, help for the helpless, friendship for the friendless, healing for the sick, sight for the blind, and eternal life for everyone who would put their trust in him.

On television, the top story changes from day to day, but from Heaven I am still broadcasting the same good news. Jesus is still my greatest headline. He is still changing lives and working miracles.

Spread the news!

God
=== =========

THE ROOM CALLED HEAVEN

Jesus said to her, "I am the resurrection and the life. He who believes in me will live, even though he dies."

| John | 11:25 |

My Child,

>What if you got a call today about the death of somebody you love? You'd probably rather not think about that. But one day you'll have to deal with death, because death is a part of life.

But death is not the end for people who believe in me. It's like a doorway between a room called Earth and a room called Heaven.

On earth there are many beautiful things, but there is also trouble and pain. But life in Heaven is only good. It is filled with unending beauty, joy, and peace. You don't get to Heaven by being good enough; you get there only by believing in Jesus. He is the key to the door of Heaven.

Your forever Father,

God

=== =========

E-mail from God for Kids

SING A SONG THAT'S ALL YOUR OWN

Sing to the Lord a new song;
sing to the Lord, all the earth.
Sing to the Lord, praise his name; proclaim
his salvation day after day.

Psalm **96:1-2**

My Child,

>Think of all the original things I have put in my world. Every leaf is different from every other leaf; every snowflake has its own design. And what about you? You are not like anybody else who has ever lived. Hold out your hand and look at your fingerprints. You have ten originals!

I love original things. That's why I want you to praise me with a song that is all your own. I have given you the creativity to make up a song that no one has ever sung before. Wait until you are all alone with me, and then try it. Even if you think you can't sing, give it a shot. Don't be shy. I will love it, no matter what it sounds like.

The Creator of Creativity,

God
=== =========

DON'T LIVE TO PLEASE OTHER PEOPLE

The Lord is with me; I will not be afraid.
What can man do to me?

| | | | ▼ | Psalm | 118:6 | ▼ | | | | |

Dear Child,

>It's funny how some people get so worried about what other people think of them. They dress a certain way to please their friends. They talk and think and act just like everyone else in the crowd so they will fit in. They are afraid to step out and have their own ideas.

I want to set you free from living to please other people. I want you to be so sure of my love and my approval that you really don't care what the others think. I want you to have your own style instead of copying someone else's. I want you to try some things that you enjoy instead of always doing what everyone else is doing.

Let my opinion be the one you value. I like your style!

Your Loving Father,

God
=== =========

E-mail from God for Kids

My people are destroyed from lack of knowledge.

| Hosea | 4:6 |

Dear Child,

>Before a soldier goes into battle, he goes to boot camp where he learns everything he needs to know about fighting a war. That way, when he goes out on the battlefield, he will have the knowledge he needs to win.

Sometimes walking through life can feel a little bit like being in a war. There are so many things that can get you down and defeat you. Because I love you, I want you to be prepared. I want you to know everything about being a winner on the battlefield of life. Read the Bible; join a church with a good youth program; and pray to me about everything. I will give you the knowledge you need to live the victory.

Your Commanding Officer,

God
=== =========

DON'T JUST KNOW IT—DO IT!

Now that you know these things, you will be blessed if you do them.

John 13:17

My Child,

>There's a big difference between knowing something and doing it. Just because you have read a lot of books about astronauts flying through space doesn't mean you have flown there yourself. Just because you have read about the geniuses who design computers doesn't mean you can design one. Just because you have watched the Olympics on television doesn't make you an Olympic champion.

Jesus came to earth telling people how to live. But he did more than talk about right living. He lived that way too. I want you to read about Jesus in the Bible. I want you to know what he told his disciples to do. But I want you to do more than just read about those things. I also want you to do them.

The Lord of Action,

God

=== =========

E-mail from God for Kids

A BIG PROMISE

God appeared to Solomon and said to him, "Ask for whatever you want me to give you." Solomon answered God... "Give me wisdom and knowledge, that I may lead this people, for who is able to govern this great people of yours?"

2 Chronicles | 1:7-8,10

Dear child,

>When Solomon became king of Israel, I told him I'd give him anything he asked for. That's a pretty big promise, right? If I told you I'd give you anything you asked for, what would it be? More money, more stuff, more friends?

Solomon asked for something that would bring lots of good things into his life. He asked me for wisdom. Being wise is not the same as being smart. Smart people make good grades on tests. Wise people make good choices in life.

So did I give Solomon what he asked for? You bet I did! And he became one of Israel's best kings.

Ask me for wisdom, my child, and I'll give you what you ask for.

The wisdom-giver,

God

=== =========

MOUNTAINS WILL MOVE

Jesus replied, "I tell you the truth, if you have faith and do not doubt...you can say to this mountain, 'Go, throw yourself into the sea,' and it will be done."

Matthew 21:21

My child,

>A prayer of faith is more than just a wish. It has muscle power. Jesus told his disciples that if they prayed with enough faith, they could move mountains.

What "mountains" would you like to move today? Maybe you're in a new school and you don't have a single friend yet. That's a problem that can seem as big as a mountain, I know. Start praying now for one new friend. As you pray, don't just sit in a corner looking glum. Work with me. Smile. Open your heart to what I'm going to do. Believe.

Also, as you pray, don't look at the mountain of fear and loneliness you're feeling. Instead, look at me. Remember, I'm the God who made mountains, and I'm the God who can move them.

Your Moving Company,

God
=== ==========

E-mail from God for Kids

FRIENDS IN HIGH PLACES

Let us then approach the throne of grace with confidence, so that we may receive mercy and find grace to help us in our time of need.

Hebrews **4:16**

My child,

>When Abraham Lincoln was president, he met with the most important people in the world. But often Lincoln's little boy Taddy would burst into the presidential office wanting to tell his dad something. Though some fathers might have fussed at such childish interruptions, President Lincoln never did. He would usually stop the meeting, scoop little Taddy up on his lap, and introduce the boy to his important guest.

I am a Dad like Lincoln was. I want you to burst in on me any time of night or day. I'll put everything else on hold. I'll scoop you up on my lap and talk with you for as long as you need me. So don't hold back. Run into your Daddy's arms.

I love you,

God

=== ==========

THE FOUNTAIN OF YOUTH

Praise the Lord, O my soul, and forget not all his benefits . . . who satisfies your desires with good things so that your youth is renewed like the eagle's.

Psalm **103:2,5**

Dear Child,

>Many early explorers went looking for the Fountain of Youth. They believed that if they discovered youth-renewing waters, they'd be rich.

I am like a fountain of youth for your mind and spirit. I have the ability to breathe new life into tired, defeated attitudes. I can touch you when you feel like giving up and give you the excitement of a fresh start. I can take a person of any age and give that person the hope and amazement of a little kid on Christmas morning. Getting to know me is like drinking every day from miracle waters.

Your Fountain of Youth,

God

=== =========

E-mail from God for Kids

FAMILY REUNION

Every day they continued to meet together.... They broke bread in their homes and ate together with glad and sincere hearts, praising God and enjoying the favor of all the people. And the Lord added to their number daily those who were being saved.

Acts 2:46-47

Dear Child,

>When early Christians got together, they often met in homes. There was no choir, no pulpit, no right way to do things. Believers prayed to the same heavenly Father—me. That made them a family. They celebrated the fact that Jesus had arisen from the dead. Most of them lived hard lives. When they got together, they encouraged each other. Everyone spoke. Everyone prayed and sang. Everyone took part.

Some churches today turn their Sunday services into a show. People come in and sit on padded seats in air-conditioned "theaters" called sanctuaries. They just sit back and watch what's happening up front. Sometimes I want to shout, "Wake up, people! I'm here. I'm real. I love you. This is not a show—it's a party. It's a family reunion!"

Father of the family,

God
=== =========

STAY IN TOUCH

Then you will call upon me and come and pray to me, and I will listen to you.

| Jeremiah | 29:12 |

My Child,

>Long ago when the West was being settled, it was hard for people to stay in touch. The Pony Express was an early mail service that used mailmen on horseback to carry letters. Later the telegraph sent messages by wire. The invention of the telephone allowed people to talk across the miles. Today with faxes, e-mail, and cell phones, staying in touch is easy and quick.

But staying in touch with me is the easiest, quickest, most awesome method of communication ever thought up. You can pray to me anytime, anywhere. You can send up a few words or a song or even just a wordless longing or feeling. I'll hear you and understand. I'll speak back in quiet heart whispers only you can hear.

Stay in touch,

God

=== =========

E-mail from God for Kids

THROUGH A SMOKY GLASS

Now we see but a poor reflection as in a mirror; then we shall see face to face. Now I know in part; then I shall know fully, even as I am fully known.

 1 Corinthians   13:12

My Child,

>I know that you have lots of questions about why things happen the way they do. Why do people get cancer? Why are there hungry people in the world? Or why did your friend have to move to a different town?

On earth there will always be unanswered questions. It's almost like looking at a movie through a piece of smoky glass. The action looks foggy. The story is unclear. But someday when you get to Heaven, you'll look right into my eyes. Then you'll be able to ask me any question you ever wanted to ask. And all of my answers will make all of your questions evaporate. Finally, it will all make sense. But until you know my answers, I want you to trust that I am in control and that I know what I'm doing.

Hold on!

God
=== =========

NOTHING IS TOO HARD

Ah, Sovereign Lord, you have made the heavens and the earth by your great power and outstretched arm. Nothing is too hard for you.

| Jeremiah | 32:17 |

My child,

>Once there was a girl named Joni who lived in California. She was pretty and smart and athletic and popular. She had everything. Then one day she broke her neck in a diving accident. When she found out she would never be able to use her arms or legs again, Joni wondered how her life could ever have any meaning again.

This is a true story, and here's what really happened. Joni put her life in my hands and let me do great things through her. Today she paints incredible pictures by holding a paintbrush in her teeth. She has a wonderful husband named Ken. She travels all over the world telling people about me. Even when everything seems to fall apart, I can make your life amazing. Nothing is impossible if you let me help you.

Trust me with your life,

God
=== =========

E-mail from God for Kids

WHAT CONTROLS YOUR MOODS?

I've learned by now to be quite content whatever my circumstances. I'm just as happy with little as with much, with much as with little. I've found the recipe for being happy whether full or hungry, hands full or hands empty. Whatever I have, wherever I am, I can make it through anything in the One who makes me who I am.

 Philippians 4:12–13 | THE MESSAGE

My Child,

>What controls your moods? Are you in a good mood when it's sunny and a bad mood when it rains? Are you in a good mood when you're eating out at a restaurant but in a bad mood when you're having leftovers at home? Are you in a good mood when you're with a friend but in a bad mood when you're with your little sister?

Listen. You can't control the weather. You can't always control where you eat or whom you get to hang out with. But you *can* control your mood. You can find an unchanging good mood when you choose to focus on my unchanging love. Then, rain or shine, tacos or meat loaf, friend or sister, you'll be content.

Your Unchanging Father,

God
=== =========

BE GRATEFULLY SATISFIED

Be content with what you have.

Hebrews	13:5

Dear Child,

>Once, a boy gave his old racing bike to his younger brother. The younger brother was thrilled. He loved the smooth ride of the racing bike, and he didn't even care that it was scratched. He rode that old racing bike every day.

Then the younger brother's best friend got a shiny, new racing bike. The minute the younger brother saw the new bike, he stopped appreciating his hand-me-down bike. He began to notice every scratch and nick on it, and before long he "had" to have a new one.

The younger brother discovered the sin of coveting—wanting what someone else has. Coveting makes you greedy and ungrateful and unhappy. I want you to avoid coveting and be grateful for the good things that you have.

Be content with what you have,

God

=== =========

E-mail from God for kids

PORTRAIT OF A CHRISTIAN

They are ... the work of my hands,
for the display of my splendor.

Isaiah	60:21

My child,

>What if I painted a portrait of the kind of Christian I'm making you into? What would you see in my painting?

You'd see eyes full of laughter that shine with hope for the future. You'd see hands that reach out with the care and compassion of Jesus. You'd see arms willing to embrace other people—the ones who are popular and the ones who are not. You'd see feet willing to go wherever necessary to do the work of my kingdom.

You'd see someone kind enough to forgive others and humble enough to forgive himself—someone big enough to hold on to my promises and small enough to need my care. You'd see a warrior, a child, a prophet, and a worshipper. You'd see someone I love with all of my heart.

You'd see you,

God

=== =========

GIVE YOUR SOUL A PEP TALK

Why are you downcast, O my soul? Why so disturbed within me? Put your hope in God.

| Psalm | 42:5 |

Dear Child,

>Do you ever wake up feeling rotten—feeling like giving up on the day before it even starts? When David, the psalm writer, felt rotten, he would give his soul a pep talk. He'd say, "Soul, what's the problem? Why are you so upset? God's on the job. Trust him."

On your rotten mornings, first try to figure out what's really bugging you. Maybe some guy acted like a jerk to you yesterday. Maybe you forgot to study for a test. Whatever it is, feeling sorry for yourself is no help. So why not try David's remedy? Give your soul a pep talk. Say, "Soul, snap out of it! God loves you, and he's waiting to help you. Stop griping and start trusting."

Make today count,

God

=== =========

E-mail from God for Kids

HE IS WHO HE IS

We have seen and testify that the Father has sent his Son to be the Savior of the world.

| 1 John | 4:14 |

My child,

>Some people in Jesus' day wanted the kind of Savior who would gallop in on a huge horse with a sharp sword and wipe out the whole Roman government. Instead, they got a quiet, humble man who walked from town to town followed by poor people and sinners and was crucified like a thief.

Today some people want a Savior who will answer their prayers with bigger paychecks, more expensive cars, and an easy life. But he's still the same Savior—the one who says the first will be last, the strongest will be the weakest, and the rich man will have a hard time getting into Heaven.

Jesus will never be what the world tries to make of him. He is who he is—your Savior, your Friend, and your Lord.

Follow him,

God

=== =========

THE RESCUE

The greatest of these is love.

1 Corinthians | **13:13**

My child,

>Once a man took a trip with his wife and children on his beautiful new sailboat. He carefully charted a course across open waters to a distant island. Even though weather forecasts had been good, an unexpected storm blew in and turned the man's dream trip into a nightmare. Huge waves crashed over his boat and sank it. He and his family members were clinging to a rubber life raft. At that moment, the man cared nothing for the boat. His only prayer was, "Lord, save my family."

Suddenly, through blinding rain, a coastguard rescue boat approached. The crew bravely pulled the man's loved ones out of the water one by one. With his family safe around him, the man praised me. In that moment, he knew what really mattered.

Don't wait for a crisis to discover what's important, my child. Love is what matters most in life.

Your Loving Father,

God

=== =========

E-mail from God for Kids

THE MAN WHO PRAYED FOR PRISONERS

To all who received him, to those who believed in his name, he gave the right to become children of God.

| John | 1:12 |

My child,

>Once there was a man who prayed for prisoners, asking me each day to help those who were locked in a cruel, dark place because of their sins. One day the man could not bear to stay outside any longer. He asked if he could spend a year living as a prisoner, though he had not broken any laws. For one year the man ate prison food, dressed in prison clothes, and slept in a prison cell. The prisoners never knew who he was, but they saw his kindness and his faith. And the man led many of those prisoners to a new life in me.

Jesus loved the world you live in so much that he could not bear to stay outside of it. Like the man who prayed for prisoners, he chose to enter a world of sin, even though he was sinless. Because Jesus entered into your world, he was able to lead people to a new life with me. Have you received him, my child?

Your Heavenly Father,

God

=== ==========

STAY PLUGGED IN

I am the vine; you are the branches. If a man remains in me and I in him, he will bear much fruit; apart from me you can do nothing.

| John | 15:5 |

Dear Child,

>If you break a branch off of a grapevine, the branch will shrivel up and die. It won't be able to make leaves or grapes anymore.

Jesus is like the grapevine, and you are like the branch. If you stay attached to him, his love can flow through you like the sap flows through the vine. And you will produce great things in your life. You'll have plenty of love and energy to help other people. You'll have wisdom and peace and a reason for living.

But if you cut yourself off from Jesus, you're choosing to die spiritually. And the great things that I want to do in your life will never happen. So stay connected to Jesus, my child.

Lord of the Vineyard,

God

E-mail from God for Kids

for nothing is impossible with God.

| Luke | 1:37 |

My Child,

>I'm excited about the amazing things you're going to do in your life. I can't wait to see the awesome difference you're going to make in the world. Maybe you're thinking, *What kind of amazing things can I do? What kind of awesome difference can I make? I'm just a kid.*

You don't have to be voting age before you qualify for awesome stuff in my kingdom. Young people have done some world-changing things. Mary was a very young girl when she made a journey to Bethlehem and became the mother of Jesus. Joshua was a young guy when he blew on a trumpet and knocked down the walls of Jericho. What Joshua and Mary had in common was faith in me. When you have faith, nothing is impossible, no matter what your age is.

The Lord with No Limits,

God
=== =========

SAILORS AND SALVATION

If you confess with your mouth Jesus as Lord, and believe in your heart that God raised Him from the dead, you will be saved; for with the heart a person believes, resulting in righteousness, and with the mouth he confesses, resulting in salvation.

Romans **10:9-10** NASB

My child,

>People can talk about boats all they want. They can learn about ocean tides, wind currents, and sail positions. They can learn about boat building and even dress like sailors. But if they never get on a boat, pull up the anchor, and head out to sea, they will never be true sailors.

The same is true of your Christian faith. You join a church, go to Sunday school every Sunday, and learn all about me. You can hear about a God who looks after you and loves you. You can even wear Christian T-shirts and hang out with Christian friends. But if you don't ever step out in faith and ask me to be your Lord, if you don't ask my Son, Jesus, to be your Savior, then you'll never be a real Christian. A Christian is someone who has given his or her life to Jesus. Only you and I know whether you have done that. So don't stand on the shore pretending to be sailing on the seas of the Christian life. Step out in faith. Don't just know about me; know me.

Your Lord and Savior,

God

=== =========

E-mail from God for Kids

HIGH FASHION

The holy garments of Aaron shall be for his sons after him, that in them they may be anointed and ordained.

Exodus 29:29

My child,

>Have you ever gone into your parents' closet and looked at some of the old clothes they used to wear? Some of them look just plain weird. It's hard to believe that it used to be cool to wear those clothes. The truth is that, on earth, what is cool and in style today will change tomorrow. Things that are the latest in style or technology will be outdated in a matter of years or sometimes even months.

But my truth is different. It never goes out of style. From the beginning of time, people have worshipped me, reaching out to their Creator, dressing their hearts in praise. When I showed myself to the Israelites thousands of years ago, they worshipped my name, "Yahweh." For two thousand years, people have known and worshiped my Son, Jesus Christ. They have worshiped me while they were dressed in Jewish robes or bell-bottom jeans. They have worshipped me as they were riding on donkeys or driving BMW motorcycles. I am the one true God. So don't follow fashions; follow me. I will never change.

The One Who's Always in Style,
God

=== =========

THE BEAUTIFUL PEOPLE

Charm is deceptive, and beauty is fleeting;
but a [person] who fears the
Lord is to be praised.

| Proverbs | 31:30 |

My Child,

>Your looks don't make you a beautiful person. Even though television and magazine ads try to make you think that looks are everything, they aren't.

Think about the person who has meant the most to you, the person who loved you the most, the one who has always been there for you. Maybe it was your mom or dad, your grandmother, or a close friend. What made that person so important to you? Was it the person's looks? Probably not. What matters most, what makes a person worthwhile and important to others, is much deeper than looks. What matters is love—the way a person loves me and the way a person loves others.

So if you want to be one of the beautiful people, don't try looking better. Try loving better.

The One Who Sees Your True Beauty,

God
=== =========

E-mail from God for Kids

YOUR DAILY STRENGTH

Sing to him, sing praise to him; tell of all his wonderful acts. Glory in his holy name; let the hearts of those who seek the Lord rejoice. Look to the Lord and his strength; seek his face always.

| 1 Chronicles | 16:9-11 |

My Child,

>When you eat, you don't just eat once and then you're full for the rest of your life. When you sleep, you don't just get one full night's sleep and then you're ready to go with no sleep forever. I didn't make you that way.

In the same way, when you became a Christian, you weren't "fixed" forever. I didn't design you with your own spiritual fuel that never runs out. I created you to come to me every day and ask me to give you strength, to guide you, and to show you love. When you come to me for this daily recharge, I'll give you the supernatural energy you need to live your life for me. Don't run out of fuel. Come and refill.

Your Power and Strength,

God

=== =========

PUTTING IT ALL TOGETHER

From there you will seek the Lord your God, and you will find Him if you search for Him with all your heart and all your soul. When you are in distress and all these things have come upon you, in the latter days you will return to the Lord your God and listen to His voice.

Deuteronomy 4:29-30 NASB

My child,

>Living your life without me is like trying to put the pieces of a jigsaw puzzle together while you're blindfolded. You can't see where the pieces of your life should go, and nothing makes sense. Once you begin to know me and my Son, Jesus, the blindfold comes off. Then you start to understand things you never could before. Piece by piece, your life starts coming together. It starts making sense.

Keep coming to me every day for direction, my child. Trying to live the Christian life without me is like trying to finish that puzzle without looking at the picture on the box. The more you pray, the more clearly you see the overall picture. The more you read the Bible, the more you'll understand my plan for your life.

The One Who Pieces You Together,

God

=== ==========

E-mail from God for Kids

THE KEY TO HAPPINESS

Make sure that your character is free from the love of money, being content with what you have; for He Himself has said, "I will never desert you, nor will I ever forsake you."

Hebrews | **13:5** NASB

My Child,

>If you live your life thinking that you'll only be happy once you lose weight or make perfect grades in school or make the first-string team, then you are bound to be disappointed sooner or later. That's because you're putting your hopes in things that aren't designed to bring you true happiness.

True happiness doesn't come from what you have or don't have. It comes from your relationship with me and my Son, Jesus.

I'm not saying that you shouldn't go for the best things in life. I just want you to know your happiness will never come from what you own or what you achieve. Get to know me, and you will find the happiness you're looking for.

The Way to Happiness,

God

=== ==========

STUBBED TOES AND CUTTING YOURSELF OFF

If a man does not repent, He will sharpen His sword; He has bent His bow and made it ready. He has dug a pit and hollowed it out, and has fallen into the hole which he made.

Psalm 7:12,15 NASB

My Child,

If you stubbed your toe, would you get so mad about it that you'd cut your toe off? That would be nuts! Instead of doing that, you would clean it, put a Band-Aid on it, and try to avoid stubbing it again.

Unfortunately, many times when people sin, rather than turning to me for healing, they cut themselves off from me by saying "What's the point? I'm just no good. I'll just wallow in my sin a little while."

I know that it's hard to live the Christian life. But when you sin, don't beat yourself up about it. Don't cut yourself off. No amount of sin can stop my love. When you sin, turn to me and honestly tell me you're sorry. Ask for my strength and my help, and I'll start you on your way again.

Your Healer,

God

E-mail from God for Kids

SKATEBOARDS AND SPORTS CARS

*But you will receive power when
the Holy Spirit comes on you.*

| Acts | 1:8 |

My Child,

>Did you ever make a New Year's resolution and tell yourself, "I'm going to try to be a better person"? That was a good goal to set for yourself, and you probably acted a little bit better—at least for a while.

There's nothing wrong with trying to change yourself all by yourself. It's just not the best way to make a change. It's like trying to get to a great place on a skateboard when I've given you a sports car to drive in.

My Holy Spirit will give you supernatural power to help you be the person I want you to be—not just to act a little better for a while, but to be totally changed on the inside. If you hand over your life to me and ask for my help, you will begin to see amazing changes—the kind of changes you could never make on your own.

Any time you're ready to see what I'm talking about, get off the skateboard of your own strength and let my Holy Spirit-powered sports car take you to a whole new place.

The One Who Changes You,

God
=== ==========

BE YOURSELF

What is desirable in a man is his kindness,
and it is better to be a poor
man than a liar.

Proverbs | **19:22** NASB

My Child,

>If an actor does a great job at playing a part in a movie, the audience will respect the actor for doing a good acting job. But in real life, when a person pretends to be someone else, it is a pathetic lie.

I know that it is tempting sometimes to pretend to be someone you aren't, to stretch the truth, to make yourself appear better than you are. But if someone else is so impressed with your lies that he wants to hang out with you, you haven't really gained a friend. Why not? Because it's your lies that person likes, not your real self.

If you will just be yourself, then the friends you make will be truly yours, and the freedom you feel will be worth it. Don't act; just be yourself.

The One Who Loves You As You Are,

God

E-mail from God for Kids

If my people, who are called by my name, will humble themselves and pray and seek my face and turn from their wicked ways, then will I hear from heaven and will forgive their sin and will heal their land.

 2 Chronicles | 7:14

My Child,

>I want you to pray for my Spirit to sweep over your school. I'm not just talking about going to a fifteen-minute formal prayer meeting at the Christian club meeting. That's an awesome place to start. But I want you to pray every day for the kids at your school who need me in their lives.

I want to move into the lives of your schoolmates in a way that will blow your mind. I want to heal the people who have had their hearts broken and who have lost their innocence. I want to teach the bullies about the love of Jesus. I want to teach the kids who don't fit in about my total acceptance. I want to use you to help me make these things happen.

Pray for my Holy Spirit to do radical things in your school. Don't give up. Keep praying for your friends and your enemies until they can pray for themselves. I will hear your prayer and answer.

The One Who Does Great Things,

God

=== =========

MY STRENGTH IN WEAKNESS

"Neither this man nor his parents sinned," said Jesus, "but this happened so that the work of God might be displayed in his life."

| John | 9:3 |

My Child,

>Sometimes if a person is weak or has a lot of problems, people wonder what that person did to deserve all the bad stuff. But I can take bad things and turn them into something good. When a weak person can't handle a heavy situation, I can come in with my strength and lift the hard stuff off of that weak person's shoulders.

Do you feel weak in some areas? Are you clumsy and not athletic? Is schoolwork always hard for you? Do you wish you had more friends? Turn those weak areas over to me. I'm the God who helped a boy named David slay a giant. I helped a boy named Solomon, who asked for wisdom, become the wisest man in the world. I helped an unholy woman named Mary Magdalene become a holy woman of God. I helped a stuttering man named Moses become the mighty leader of my people. None of these people were the best at what they set out to do. But they turned their weaknesses over to me, and I changed them. Turn over your life to me, and I will work through you too.

Your Strength,

God

E-mail from God for Kids

SOAK UP THE GOOD STUFF

Blessed is the man who does not walk in the counsel of the wicked or stand in the way of sinners or sit in the seat of mockers. But his delight is in the law of the Lord, and on his law he meditates day and night. He is like a tree planted by streams of water, which yields its fruit in season and whose leaf does not wither. Whatever he does prospers.

Psalm   1:1-3

My Child,

>An empty sponge will soak up any liquid it comes in contact with. If it gets around stinky vinegar, it will soak that up. If it gets around pure spring water, it will soak that up. But once it's full, it can't soak up anything else until it is wrung out.

You're kind of like a sponge. I made you empty so that you could soak up all of my good stuff. I know sometimes it's tempting to hang out with the "bad" crowd and soak up the bad stuff that they do. But I don't want you to get so full of stinking vinegar that you miss out on my pure water. I want to fill you with love, kindness, happiness, and real peace. Let me help you wring out all the bad stuff you've soaked up. Then pray and ask me to fill you with my Holy Spirit. Once you're filled with my goodness, you won't want anything else.

The Pure Water,

God

=== =========

CASTLES IN THE SAND

For the Lord watches over the way of the righteous, but the way of the wicked will perish.

| Psalm | 1:6 |

My Child,

>Have you ever gone to the beach and built a sand castle right next to the water? What happens? At the end of the day, the tide rises, and the water wrecks the castle.

Living your life for the wrong reasons is kind of the same way. Even if you end up making a lot of money and getting lots of stuff, if you don't live your life for me, then all that stuff won't matter in the end. It will be washed away like that sand castle. But if you trust in my Son, Jesus, and live your life for him, then your life is like building a strong house on solid ground that the water can't move. If you really want your life to count for something in the end, build a life that will last.

Your Solid Foundation,

God
===   =========

E-mail from God for kids

DIAMONDS

"Then your fame went forth among the nations on account of your beauty, for it was perfect because of My splendor which I bestowed on you," declares the Lord God.

Ezekiel 16:14 NASB

My child,

>Have you ever looked really closely at a diamond? When you shine a light on a diamond, it is one of the most beautiful sights in the world. Sometimes it can even look like the diamond is shining by itself. But if you put a diamond in a dark room, it doesn't shine by itself at all. That's because it can only reflect the light that shines on it.

The same is true with you. I have made you to shine, but you can't shine by yourself. You need to place yourself in the light of my love. Then, when I am shining on you, you will be able to reflect my light to the world. When you do that, you will be what I created you to be: one of the most beautiful things on earth.

The Light of Love,

God

=== =========

DON'T COOL OFF

Stir up Your power and come to save us!
O God, restore us and cause Your face
to shine upon us, and we will be saved.

Psalm 80:2-3 NASB

My Child,

>Have you ever made some really good hot chocolate, but when you finally got around to drinking it, it had gotten kind of cold? That can be a bummer.

I know the way that feels, because I created you to be on fire for me. And it bums me out when I see you kind of cooled off and not caring about God things.

If you have gotten cold in your Christian faith, I want to heat you up again. But nothing gets heated up away from the stove. You've got to come to me, the source of spiritual heat. Just admit that you've gotten cold and ask me to heat you up again with my Spirit. When you feel that excitement for God things bubbling inside you, you will know that your faith is warming up. Don't let your love get cold again.

Your Spiritual Fire,

God

=== =========

E-mail from God for Kids

THREAD THAT NEEDLE

Nobody should seek his own good, but the good of others. . . . Even as I try to please everybody in every way. For I am not seeking my own good but the good of many, so that they may be saved.

1 Corinthians 10:24,33

My Child,

>If you got a rip in your favorite shirt and you knew how to sew, you'd want to fix it, wouldn't you? If I gave you a needle and a spool of thread, you wouldn't put them in a drawer and never use them. You'd use them to mend your shirt, wouldn't you?

There is pain and brokenness all around you. Friends of yours may be hurting and need help. They may need somebody to talk to. You could be the very person I use to mend the hearts of your friends. I also can use you to help total strangers. I have given you gifts to share. I've also given you the love of Jesus and the power of the Holy Spirit so that you can do your part to help mend your broken world.

If you don't use your gifts to mend your world, it's just like putting the needle and thread in a drawer and not trying to fix the shirt. It's time to care for more than what you want and what you need. I want you to start looking for other people in your life who need help. Thread that needle, and let's get to work!

The One Who Helps You,
God

=== ==========

THE SERVANT OF ALL

Now we who are strong ought to bear the weaknesses of those without strength and not just please ourselves. Each of us is to please his neighbor for his good, to his edification. For even Christ did not please Himself; but as it is written, "The reproaches of those who reproached You fell on Me."

Romans **15:1-3 NASB**

My child,

>Have you ever heard the saying, "You've got to look out for number one (yourself)"? That saying is not in my Bible. It is a saying used by self-centered people who spend all their time and energy looking out for their own needs. But Jesus spent his time on earth doing things for others. When you live like Jesus, you become what I created you to be—a servant.

Television ads hardly ever sound like the Bible. The ads say, "Do something nice for yourself; you're worth it" or "You deserve everything you want and more." Imagine a television commercial that tried to sell you something by saying, "This product will make you the lowest on the ladder, the servant of all around you." The person who came up with that commercial would be fired.

But Jesus became the lowest on the ladder so that you could be lifted up. If you live your life like he did, you will be amazed at how much better it feels to serve others than to just grab a lot of stuff for yourself. Give it a try.

The Greatest Servant,

God

E-mail from God for Kids

LOVE AND MERCY NEVER TASTED SO SWEET

The Lord's lovingkindnesses indeed never cease, for His compassions never fail. They are new every morning; great is Your faithfulness.

Lamentations 3:22-23 NASB

My Child,

>Have you ever gotten a really good milkshake? It tastes so good that you don't ever want it to end. But even though you may try to make it last, when it's gone, it's gone. It's normal to want good things to last forever. And it's also normal to have a fear of their running out.

Well, my love and forgiveness for you are the sweetest, most incredible things you will ever know. My love and mercy taste as good to your heart and your soul as a really good milkshake tastes to your mouth and your stomach. And the best part is, you don't ever need to worry about them running out. As fast as you can receive them, I will keep pouring them out. So drink in my love and mercy.

Giving You the Good Stuff,

God

=== =========

SCREEN SAVERS OF THE HEART

As for me, I shall behold Your face in righteousness; I will be satisfied with Your likeness when I awake.

Psalm **17:15 NASB**

My Child,

>Do you have a screen saver on your computer? You know, when you don't move the mouse or type anything in for a while, the computer goes into sleep mode and the screen saver comes on. Even though the computer is still plugged in and turned on, it's asleep. Until you hit a key or move the mouse, the computer is useless to you.

The same thing can happen to Christians. It's possible to "fall asleep" in your faith. It's not that you stop believing in me or that you completely unplug your Christianity; it's just that you can shut down any real interactive contact and simply go through the motions. It's obvious to me and to you when you go into a spiritual sleep mode. There's a lack of activity—a lack of excitement in your prayers, a lack of caring for others, a feeling of distance between you and me.

If you're in this spiritual sleep mode, it's time to come alive again. Pray to me and ask me to revive you. I will hit the key of your heart, and you will spring to life.

It's time to wake up,

God

=== =========

E-mail from God for Kids

We know that God causes all things to work together for good to those who love God, to those who are called according to His purpose.

Romans | **8:28 NASB**

My Child,

>Pearls are one of the most beautiful jewels on earth. But the way they are formed is not a glamorous process. It starts with an oyster, a very plain, slimy animal that lives in a shell. If a large grain of sand gets into that shell, over time it can become a pearl. Here's how that happens: The oyster surrounds the sand with a coating called *nacre* that hardens. In time that coated grain of sand can turn into a beautiful pearl.

In the same way that sand gets into the oyster, hard things can come into your life. Those things can irritate you or really bring you down. But I can use those bad things to bring good things into your life. Making a bad grade can motivate you to study harder so you learn more. Getting your feelings hurt can help you better understand other people who have hurt feelings. The death of a family member can be the very thing that leads you to me.

When tough stuff enters your world, don't just gripe about it. Instead, start to look for ways that I might want to turn that sand into a beautiful pearl.

The One Who Brings Good from Bad,
God

=== ==========

FILLING AND FUELING

May the God of hope fill you with all joy and peace as you trust in him, so that you may overflow with hope by the power of the Holy Spirit.

| Romans | 15:13 |

My Child,

>Cars don't run on water. Even though you can fill up a gas tank with water and it will be full of something, it won't be full of what that car really needs to get going.

That's true of you too. You are like a tank that can be filled with lots of things. But there's a difference between being filled and being fueled. Only I can fuel you with what you need to function as a total person. Friends can't do that. Money can't do that. Owning a lot of stuff can't do that. Only I can. So empty your tank of whatever you've filled it with, and ask me to fuel you with the power you need.

Fill 'er up,

God

=== =========

E-mail from God for Kids

THE ROOTS GROW DEEPER

Not only this, but we also exult in our tribulations, knowing that tribulation brings about perseverance; and perseverance, proven character; and proven character, hope.

Romans | 5:3-4 nasb

My Child,

>During very dry weather, when there is no rain, trees send their roots deeper and deeper into the soil to find the stuff they need to live. The deeper the roots go, the stronger the tree becomes. With its roots firmly anchored in the ground, the tree can't be blown over in strong winds.

Hard things that happen in your life can be like dry weather in the life of a tree. They can make you put the roots of your faith down deep into your relationship with me. The deeper the roots of your faith grow, the stronger you will become. The closer you get to me, the more you will find all the stuff you need to live and survive. Soon you'll be strong enough to make it through anything. So press into me when the times get tough. I'll strengthen you.

The Soil of Your Faith,

God

=== ==========

NOW THAT IS COOL

God saw all that he had made,
and it was very good.

| Genesis | 1:31 |

My child,

>Whenever you make something really cool, don't you just want to gather all your friends around and show them? You're proud of what you made and sometimes even a little bit surprised at how cool it is. That's how I am with you. I made you just the way I wanted. Then I stood back and looked at what I made and said, "That is the coolest thing I have ever seen. I want everybody to see the awesome person I've made you to be."

I know everything about you. I know the best thing about you and even the things that you think are wrong with you. I want you to know that I don't think there's anything wrong with you. I couldn't be any more proud of you. I love you for exactly who you are. Just know that when I look at you, I stand back and say, "Now that is cool."

Your creator,

God

=== ==========

E-mail from God for kids

For the message of the cross is foolishness to those who are perishing, but to us who are being saved it is the power of God.

 1 Corinthians   1:18

My child,

>I'm not interested in whether people think I'm cool or not. I don't care whether they think I make sense to their generation. I just care that people know the truth about me.

You need to make your own decision about me, regardless of whether your friends think I'm cool or not. Do you believe that I created the heavens, the earth, everything on it, and that I created you? Do you believe that you have a need for something greater than yourself? Do you feel empty inside sometimes? Do you feel like you need something more? Do you believe that people turn their backs on me every day? Do you believe that I sent my Son, Jesus Christ, to die on the cross so that you could turn back around and have a living relationship with me? Do you believe I love you?

You need to make up your mind what you really believe, whether it's cool to believe it or not. Search your heart; search the Bible; search me out in prayer. I want you to know the truth.

The One to Believe In,
God

=== ==========

HOW DO YOU EAT YOUR M&M'S?

Now there are different kinds of gifts,
but the same Spirit.

| 1 Corinthians | 12:4 |

My Child,

>There are a lot of ways to eat a bag of M&Ms. Some people tear the bag open and put all the candy in their mouth at once. Some people eat them slowly, one by one. And some eat all the red ones first, and so on. All of them eat the M&Ms; how they eat them just depends on the personality of the eater.

There are a lot of ways to live out your Christianity. There are those people, like Peter, who are excited to do my will. They are go-getters who like to go at life all at once. Then there are people like Thomas, who like to take it a little bit slower. And there are scientific types, like Luke the doctor. There are almost as many types of Christians as there are people.

There are definitely things that all Christians should shoot for, like faith in Jesus and having a humble heart. But not every Christian is going to look or act the same. I made you a one-of-a-kind person. Don't worry about acting like somebody else's idea of what a Christian should be. Seek me, and I will show you who you were meant to be.

The Father of Uniqueness,
God

=== =========

E-mail from God for Kids

DO WHATEVER HE TELLS YOU

*His mother said to the servants, "Whatever He says to you, do it."
... Jesus said to them, "Fill the waterpots with water." So
they filled them up to the brim.... When the headwaiter tasted
the water which had become wine, and did not know where it
came from ... the headwaiter called the bridegroom.*

John   2:5,7,9 NASB

My Child,

>At a wedding, my Son, Jesus, told the servants to fill
some jars with water and take some of that water to the
headwaiter. The servants didn't know Jesus was going to
turn the water into wine. They might have felt kind of
stupid taking plain old water to the headwaiter. They
could have told Jesus, "No way." But they didn't. They did
what Jesus told them. They put their doubts on hold and
took action. And as they obeyed, the miracle was
performed. The water became wine.

I don't always give you the whole picture. Sometimes I
even tell you to do things for me that seem crazy. But if
you know it's me talking, just do what I tell you. When
you act in faith, you'll see miracles in your own life.

The One Who Speaks,

God

=== =========

GO STRAIGHT TO THEM

Therefore, if you are offering your gift at the altar and there remember that your brother has something against you, leave your gift there in front of the altar. First go and be reconciled to your brother; then come and offer your gift.

Matthew 5:23-24

My Child,

>If someone hurts your feelings, I want you to go straight to that person and talk about it. I know it's easier to talk bad about that person behind his back and avoid the confrontation. But that won't help anything. I want you to be kind and forgiving. I also want you to be brave enough to face hard situations. Many times what seems like a huge deal just turns out to be a misunderstanding. Other times it's a real problem, and you solve it by talking it out. And sometimes the other person refuses to deal with it. But if you go and talk it out the best you can, you'll know you did your part to solve the problem.

Once you start facing your problems with others, you'll have a lot less anger, a lot more trust, and a much more honest life.

The One Who Stands with You,

God
=== =========

E-mail from God for Kids

Jesus replied: "'Love the Lord your God with all your heart and with all your soul and with all your mind.' This is the first and greatest commandment. And the second is like it: 'Love your neighbor as yourself.'"

Matthew | **22:37-39**

My child,

>Of all the things I tell you in the Bible, everything can be boiled down to these two things: Love me with all of your heart, and love your neighbor as well as you love yourself.

Love is the precious treasure of Heaven given to you on earth. The more love you give out, the more you have. I want you to receive my love for you. And I want you to love me back with all of your heart. The more you love me, the more love you'll have available to give people around you.

Some people spend so much time trying to get love for themselves that they never have time to love anyone else. I want you to be so filled with my love that you are just looking for opportunities to love other people. Trust me, and I'll love others through you—even your enemies.

The Giver of Love,

God
=== =========

THE BAR IS TOO HIGH

*Charm is deceptive, and beauty is fleeting;
but a woman who fears the Lord,
she is to be praised.*

| Proverbs | 31:30 |

My child,

>There is so much pressure on kids your age to look a certain way, to act a certain way, and to live up to certain expectations. Some girls your age dress to look older, but they haven't matured yet. Some of them starve themselves to look like a model in a magazine, but they're just not that body type.

Just because a tall Olympic high jumper can leap incredibly high, that's no reason for a small fifth-grader to sit at home feeling depressed. And just because a twenty-five-year-old model looks great in a fashion magazine, that's no reason for a sixth-grader to sit at home and beat herself up for being short. Just as the high-jump bar is set too high for someone who isn't fully grown, the bar of expectations for looks is also set too high.

Let go of the expectations. Believe me; I have created you perfectly. Cut yourself some slack and love yourself for who you are.

Your creator,

God

=== ===========

E-mail from God for Kids

You are my hiding place and my shield;
I wait for Your word.

Psalm 119:114 NASB

My Child,

>Back when warriors used to fight with swords and bows and arrows, a shield was a great thing to have. With all of those sharp things coming at you, a shield could mean the difference between life and death. But having a shield wasn't enough. It had to be lifted up in order to block the swords and arrows.

I am your shield. I can protect you against all the sharp, rude things people say. I can protect your heart from getting pierced by the arrows of lies or gossip. But just like a real battle shield, you need to lift me up. How can you do this? You can lift me up by praying for my help and by trusting in me. Don't trust in anything else to guard you. I am the only shield you need. So when you need protection, lift me up, and I will protect you.

Your Shield,

God

=== =========

SHOW THE WAY

*Your word is a lamp to my feet
and a light to my path.*

Psalm | **119:105**

My child,

>If you were lost in a strange place and didn't know which way to go, wouldn't you want the most experienced guide to help you find your way? Of course you would. Growing up is like trying to find your way through an unfamiliar land. There are lots of dead ends, wrong turns, and important choices to make in life. But you don't have to make it through on your own.

I am the best guide to help you through this growing-up experience. I can keep you on track and away from danger. Not only can I get you through in one piece, I can make it more fun than any journey you've ever been on. I have given you the ultimate road map—the Bible. If you read the Bible and pray to me for guidance, things that seemed confusing will begin to make sense. Hard situations will become challenges to learn from. If you take my hand, I will lead you into a new place where life will become a joy rather than just something hard. If you feel lost in this whole growing-up thing, call on me, and I will guide you through.

Take my hand,
God

=== =========

E-mail from God for kids

For I am the Lord, who heals you.

| Exodus | 15:26 |

My child,

>If you had a disease and were dying slowly, you would want the doctor to do anything in his power to save you. That's exactly what is happening in your life. Because you are a human being, you have the condition of sin in your life. Sin is the thing that keeps you from being tight with me, and it can keep you from spending eternity with me after you die.

Because of it, you are in need of a serious operation. You need Jesus Christ, the great doctor, to come in and remove your sin. He's able to do it. He died on a cross to make a way for you to be healed. All you need to do is ask Jesus for that healing. Let him come into your life. He'll clean you up and make you well. Call on the Great Physician.

Your Father,

God
=== =========

A BROTHER'S LOVE

Walk in love, just as Christ also loved you and gave Himself up for us, an offering and a sacrifice to God as a fragrant aroma.

| | Ephesians | 5:2 NASB | |

My child,

>I want to tell you a story. There once were two brothers who loved each other very much. The brothers were about five years old when one of them became sick. The parents took both boys to the hospital, where they found that the sick brother needed a blood transfusion. They talked to the brother who was well and explained to him what they needed to do. Because he had the same blood type, they needed to take some of his blood and give it to the sick brother so he would get well.

The well brother said that he understood, and he lay down as they began to take his blood. When they were done, the well brother said quietly, "How long will it be until I die?" You see, he thought that because he had given his blood to his brother, he was going to have to die. And he had been willing to do that to make his brother well.

That's the kind of love Jesus had for you. He is the brother who loved you so much that he shed his blood and gave his life so you could live.

The One Who Sent Jesus,
God

=== =========

E-mail from God for Kids

MAKE A GOOD-STUFF LIST

Let the peace of Christ rule in your hearts, since as members of one body you were called to peace. And be thankful.

Colossians	3:15

My child,

>In the Garden of Eden, Adam and Eve had it good. Everything came easily to them, and they had no worries. But even though I had showered them with great things, they still weren't satisfied. They wanted to be gods themselves. So they chose to turn their backs on me, and I had to punish them by throwing them out of the Garden.

It's easy for people today to look back and say, "What dummies! Why couldn't they see that they had it so good?" But look at your own life. Look at all the good things in your life, and then look at how seldom you thank me. I'm not going to punish you for not saying "thank you," but you would be much happier if you did. When you're thankful for what you've been given instead of always wanting more, you'll live a happy life. So make a list of all the good stuff in your life—things such as your health, your family, your friends, a place to sleep, and food to eat. Then put your good-stuff list up where you can see it, and be thankful.

The Giver of All Good Things,
God
=== ==========

TAKE OFF THE SHADES

Set your mind on things above,
not on earthly things.

| Colossians | 3:2 |

My Child,

>You could be out on the sunniest day of the year, and if you had really dark sunglasses on, nothing would look sunny. Many people go through life never noticing how awesome life really is. They put on a bad attitude like a pair of shades. To them, it doesn't matter how many good things they have in their lives. They choose to look at the bad things instead. A bad attitude will affect everything you look at, just like the sunglasses do.

There will always be bad things and good things in your life. Many times your happiness depends on what things you choose to think about. I want you to be a person who focuses on the good things you have rather than on the bad. I want you to have a grateful attitude and thank me for the good things. Don't let a bad attitude darken your vision. Take off those negative shades and look at the light in your life.

Giver of Light,

God

=== =========

E-mail from God for Kids

I AM REAL

"I am the Alpha and the Omega," says the Lord God, "who is, and who was, and who is to come, the Almighty."

| Revelation | 1:8 |

My Child,

>I am real. Whether you choose to believe in me or not doesn't make me any less real. Whether your parents believe in me or not doesn't mean that I don't work in their lives every day. Whether your friends believe in me or not doesn't change the fact that I sent my only Son to die for each and every one of them.

What if the weatherman said that a tornado was heading straight for your house? You could just sit there, close your eyes, and refuse to believe it. But that wouldn't change the fact that you were about to be blown away.

Your choosing to believe in me makes one very big difference. When you choose to believe in me, you get to experience more and more of me in your life.

Choose to believe,

God
=== =========

TUG-OF-WAR

For our struggle is not against flesh and blood, but against the rulers, against the powers, against the world forces of this darkness, against the spiritual forces of wickedness in the heavenly places.

Ephesians **6:12 NASB**

My child,

>Have you ever played tug-of-war? You get a big thick rope and tie a ribbon in the middle. Then a team gets at each end of the rope. Each team tries to pull the ribbon over to their side. So which team wins? The strongest, most able team, of course.

Well, there is a huge tug-of-war going on inside of you. It's like you're that ribbon in the middle of the rope. I'm trying to pull you into the light, but Satan wants to pull you into the darkness. I'm trying to pull you towards friendship, joy, and peace. Satan is trying to pull you towards selfishness, sin, and worry. Sometimes you can feel this tugging in your heart. Whenever you know you should do the right thing, you can feel me pulling. But when you just don't feel like doing the right thing, or if you feel like doing something bad instead, you can feel Satan pulling.

So who wins in this tug-of-war of your heart? I am definitely the strongest and most able team, but you need to let me pull you into the light. When you feel me pulling, go with me.

The Strongest,
God

=== ==========

E-mail from God for Kids

BE CREATIVE

I have filled him with the Spirit of God in wisdom, in understanding, in knowledge, and in all kinds of craftsmanship, to make artistic designs for work in gold, in silver, and in bronze, and in the cutting of stones for settings, and in the carving of wood, that he may work in all kinds of craftsmanship.

Exodus 31:3–5 NASB

My Child,

>I have made you to be a very creative person. I have placed wonderful dreams in your heart and wonderful gifts in your hands.

Creativity is something I put in all people. Very young children love to draw. They don't care what they draw nearly as much as they simply love to create things. But as those children get older, they are told who is good at drawing and who is not good at it. The teachers and parents tell them to make things a certain way and to color within the lines. Because of that, some kids just give up on being creative. They start comparing themselves to the other kids instead of just making stuff for the joy of making it.

I don't want you to let anyone steal the joy of your creativity. I'm here to set you free from "coloring inside the lines." I am the most creative being in the world, and you are my child. So whatever you love to create, go for it and don't let anybody stop you.

The One Who Created You,
God

GET IN THE TUB

"Come now, let us reason together," says the Lord.
"Though your sins are like scarlet, they shall be
as white as snow; though they are red as
crimson, they shall be like wool."

| | Isaiah | | 1:18 | | |

My Child,

>Imagine a little boy who had been out playing in the mud. Now that kid is crusted with mud from head to toe. He needs a bath something horrible. Do you think he will be ashamed to take a bath because of how dirty he is? No way! He knows bathtubs are for getting people clean, and he'll jump into the water.

So why should you feel like you need to clean up your act before you come to me? I know the world can be a dirty place, and I know that sometimes you feel like you're covered from head to toe with the dirtiness of sin. But I'm like the bathtub. I don't expect you to be clean before you come to me. I'm here to clean you off. So come to me. Don't be embarrassed. Confess your sins. Get in the tub, and I will clean you up.

The One Who Forgives,

God
=== ==========

E-mail from God for Kids

JUST BE YOURSELF

But when Jesus heard this, He said, "It is not those who are healthy who need a physician, but those who are sick. . . . I did not come to call the righteous, but sinners."

 Matthew 9:12-13 NASB

My Child,

>I sent Jesus to love the really messed-up people, not just the ones who look like they've got it all together. If you think I'm waiting for you to dress up in your Sunday clothes and act perfect before I love you, then you're off base. I love you right now, this very second, exactly as you are. I know everything you've done right and everything you've done wrong, and I still love you completely.

What if you really loved somebody, but that person would only hang out with you once they had bathed and dressed in their best clothes and were on their best behavior? It would make you sad because when you really love somebody, you want to be with that person all the time—on good days and bad days.

That's how I feel about you. Don't feel like you have to be at your best to hang out with me. Just be yourself.

The One Who Loves You,

God
=== =========

YOU CAN'T EARN MY LOVE

By grace you have been saved through faith;
and that not of yourselves, it is the gift of God;
not as a result of works, so that no one may boast.

| Ephesians | 2:8-9 NASB |

My Child,

>You can't do anything to make me love you any less or any more. You could do all the bad stuff in the whole world, and it wouldn't make me love you any less. Sure, it would make me sad and hurt my heart, but I wouldn't love you any less.

Also, you could do all the good stuff there is to do. You could go to church seven days a week, help old ladies cross the street, give all of your money to the poor, and it wouldn't increase my love for you one bit. I would be happy for you and for those whom you helped, but I wouldn't love you any more than I already do.

You see, I already love you all the way, totally. The decisions you make show how much you love me, but they don't affect how much I love you. So if you do good deeds, do them to bless me and to bless other people. If you go to church, do it to get something out of it and to give something back. Don't do that stuff to try and make me love you more. I already love you 100 percent.

Love,
God
=== =========

E-mail from God for Kids

CHEER FOR THE STRUGGLING

Thus has the Lord of hosts said, "Dispense true justice and practice kindness and compassion each to his brother."

| Zechariah | 7:9 NASB |

My Child,

>There once was a little girl named Katrina who had a problem with stuttering when she spoke. Because of this, she was terrified to speak in front of her class. The thing that scared her most was the oral report each student had to give at the end of the year.

The year passed quickly, and the week for the reports arrived. When it was Katrina's turn, she stood nervously and began her speech. "A-A-A-A-Abrah-h-am L-L-L-Lincoln," she started. Some of her classmates began to laugh. Mrs. Jones, Katrina's teacher, scolded them, and Katrina kept going. She stuttered through her whole report. When she was finally finished, Katrina wanted to die of embarrassment, but Mrs. Jones stood to her feet and applauded. One by one, the other kids also stood and clapped for Katrina because giving her report had been the bravest thing of all.

Why do I tell you this story? Because I want you to choose what kind of person you are going to be. When you see someone who is struggling, will you laugh, or will you cheer? I want you to learn to cheer for a brave heart.

I'm cheering for you,
God

=== =========

GO TALK TO THEM

Therefore keep watch, because you do not know the day or the hour.

Matthew   25:13

My Child,

>If you found out you had one day to live and you could talk to one person before you died, whom would you call? What would you say? Maybe you would call a friend and apologize for something you did that was wrong. Maybe you would walk into the next room and tell your mom or dad how much you love them. Well, why wait until you're about to die? If you have something that you need to tell somebody, do it. Life is too short to keep important things like that to yourself.

It's funny how people walk around with all sorts of bottled-up feelings and thoughts that they should express, but they feel funny doing it. They feel afraid of what the other person will think. Love and friendship are important. People in your life need to hear from you. Go tell them how you feel.

The One Who Talks to You,

God
=== =========

E-mail from God for Kids

COMMUNION MEANS HANGING OUT TOGETHER

*God, who has called you into fellowship
with his Son Jesus Christ our Lord, is faithful.*

| 1 Corinthians | 1:9 |

My Child,

>Did you know that communion isn't just a time when you go to church and drink wine or grape juice? It isn't just the act of eating crackers or bread. Communion is a time of sharing with me. It's a time of celebrating the fact that you and I are a part of one another.

My Son, Jesus, shed his blood and sacrificed his body on the cross so we could spend time together and so there would be nothing separating us. Now, because of Jesus, we can have that together time anywhere.

I am always with you, but communion is more than that. Communion is when you make a real effort to pay attention to me, to focus your heart and mind on me. That can happen anytime, anywhere. Just talk to me. Pray and listen. Let's spend some of that communion, hang-out time together.

Your Friend,

God
=== =========

WRITE IT DOWN

Then the Lord answered me and said, "Record the vision and inscribe it on tablets."

| | Habakkuk | 2:2 NASB | |

My child,

>Do you ever have a hard time praying? Does your mind sometimes wander? If so, let me suggest something to you. Try writing your prayers down as you pray them. This doesn't work best for everybody, but if you're having trouble, give it a try.

Write out whatever's on your mind, like, "Good morning, God, it's me. I pray that you'll be with me today. I sure do love you. Thank you for loving me so much." You can also write down the names of people you pray for. Also you can write, "What do you want to tell me today, God?" Then listen for my silent words. When you feel me speaking to your heart, write down the words you hear me saying. Doing this might help you in your prayer times, and later you'll have a great record of what we talked about.

Speak plainly to me. You don't need to say, "Almighty, good, gracious, heavenly Father, I beseech thee to hear my prayers." Feel free to call me Father, Friend, or even Daddy. Be honest and be yourself. Just pray to me. And try writing it all down.

The One Who Hears Your Prayers,
God

=== =========

E-mail from God for Kids

The plans of the heart belong to man, but the answer of the tongue is from the Lord. All the ways of a man are clean in his own sight, but the Lord weighs the motives. Commit your works to the Lord and your plans will be established.

 Proverbs 16:1-3 NASB

My child,

>Do you have a plan for your life? Many people do. They say that they will make good grades in middle and high school so that they can get into a good college. They say that they will make good grades in college so that they will get a good job and make lots of money. They want lots of money so they can buy lots of stuff and so they can retire and spend the last fifteen years of their lives chasing a golf ball around or walking around with a metal detector on some tropical beach.

There's nothing so wrong with all of that, except it falls way short of my plans. A big bank account and a comfortable retirement don't compare with the things I will do in your life if you will just make following me your number one goal. I will use you to feed the starving and heal the brokenhearted. If you give your life to me 100 percent, I will fill it with meaning rather than emptiness. I'm not telling you to give up on school and have no plan. I'm telling you to seek my plan for your life. Then hold on!

It's gonna be great!

God

=== ==========

NOT JUST YOUR GIFTS

*Love the Lord your God with all your heart and
with all your soul and with all your strength.*

| | Deuteronomy | 6:5 | |

My child,

>I want to tell you a story. There once was a very shy man who had one of the most beautiful singing voices on earth. His father had been a butcher, and so, instead of becoming a singer, he took up the family business. He had a kind heart, and he made a good living. He had a deep belief in me. He taught the seventh-grade Sunday school class at his church and led several of his students into a relationship with me. He married and had four children, whom he raised to be wonderful people. He loved to sing in the shower and on the back row of the choir, but he never sang a solo.

When the man died, he went to Heaven. The day he stood before me, he asked, "Are you disappointed that I didn't become a singer?" I smiled at him and told him that his whole life had been a beautiful song of praise to me.

My child, I don't want you to get so caught up in using your gifts for me that you forget to live your whole life for me.

Praise me with your life,

God

E-mail from God for kids

KEEP YOUR FOCUS

Finally, brothers, whatever is true, whatever is noble, whatever is right, whatever is pure, whatever is lovely, whatever is admirable--if anything is excellent or praiseworthy--think about such things.

Philippians	4:8

My Child,

>A camcorder is a great way to record memorable events. You can point it at whatever you want to remember and record it. Then you can watch it later. But have you ever seen people who were so busy recording life's important moments that they forgot to live those important moments? These folks have hours and hours of tapes that they will never watch again in their lifetime. They spend every family event looking at life through the camcorder. They are so obsessed with capturing the memory that they never live the moment.

There is a lesson in this. I don't want you to live your life focused on the wrong things. You can be more worried about what you're wearing than about whether you're having a good time wearing it. You can focus so much on hanging out with the "right group" of friends that you miss a chance to make friends with someone in another group.

Keep your focus on these important things: friendship, truth, love, faith, hope, and kindness.

The One Who Helps You Focus,
God
=== ==========

THIS MOMENT IN TIME

Do not worry about tomorrow, for tomorrow will worry about itself. Each day has enough trouble of its own.

| | Matthew | 6:34 | |

My Child,

>This minute in time is all that you have. This second, while you are reading this book, is the only second you are actually alive. The past is just a bunch of used seconds stacked on top of each other. And the future is just a bunch of unused seconds waiting to happen. The funny thing is, many people spend most of their here-and-now moments feeling guilty about things that they've done in the past or worrying about things that might happen in the future. Those things aren't life. Right now is your life, and why would you want to mess it up by filling it with guilt and worries of the past and future?

If you've messed up in the past, confess your sin and let me forgive you. If you're worried about something in the future, ask me to give you courage. Then live your life guilt- and worry-free. Take joy in this moment in time because it's the only moment you really have.

The Giver of Life,

God

=== ==========

E-mail from God for Kids

DRINK THE MARROW OUT OF LIFE

I came that [you] may have life,
and have it abundantly.

John   **10:10** NASB

My child,

>When a wild animal eats its prey, it will sometimes eat all the meat and even crunch the bones and drink the marrow out of them. Now that's hungry (and kind of gross).

There's a saying about that type of hunger. People say, "Drink the marrow out of life." That means getting everything out of life that you can while you're alive. It doesn't mean to live rich or dangerously. It means to live each moment as if it really matters, because it does. Smell the flowers. Lie down in a field of grass. Climb a tree. Tell all the people you love how much they mean to you. Do something really nice for someone. Make a decision to give up worrying. Live your life for me. Don't be satisfied to sit on the couch and watch other people on television living life. Be hungry enough for life to get out there and eat it up, down to the marrow.

The Giver of Life,

God

=== =========

A MISSION FOR YOU

But when you give to the needy, do not let your left hand know what your right hand is doing, so that your giving may be in secret. Then your father, who sees what is done in secret, will reward you.

Matthew	6:3-4

My child,

>It's funny that when people do something wrong, they will try as hard as they can to hide it from everyone. But when those same people do a good deed, they practically sound a trumpet and announce, "Look what a great person I am!"

That's why I'm sending you on this mission today. I want you to do something good for someone just for the fun of doing it. And here's the hard part—I want you to do your best to keep that person from knowing you did it. It won't be a total secret. You and I will know what you have done, and we'll get a big kick out of it.

If it works out, see if you can plan other "secret missions" in the future. You will begin to love the feeling of handing out secret blessings. Now get busy. Go out and accomplish your mission.

Your Secret Agent Ally,

God

=== =========

E-mail from God for Kids

WORSHIP ME

All the earth will worship You, and will sing praises to You; they will sing praises to Your name.

| Psalm | 66:4 NASB |

My Child,

>You were created to worship me. It's like you've got a worshipping microchip in your head that says, "I must worship." But if you don't worship me, you are bound to worship something else. Just look at all the teen-idol magazines and the way people worship rock stars and sports heroes. The reason they do that is that it is totally natural for human beings to worship something they feel is high above them.

But those actors, models, musicians, and athletes are just people, and they weren't meant to be worshipped. So even if you see all of your friends worshipping one person or another and you feel tempted to join in, realize that those are just people. Choose to worship me. It's what you were made to do.

The One to Worship,

God

=== =========

DOGS AND GOD

Know that the Lord has set apart the
man for himself; the Lord will
hear when I call to him.

Psalm | 4:3

My child,

>A Labrador retriever is a dog that was bred to fetch things and bring them back to his owner. If you throw a tennis ball or a stick for a Labrador, that dog will fetch it all day long because that's what he was made to do.

I made you to have a relationship with me. When you pray and when you hang out with me, that's the most natural thing you will ever do. And once you begin to spend that time with me, you will want to do it more and more.

So go ahead and do what comes naturally. Get to know me as a friend. It's what you were made for.

The One Who Made You,

God
=== =========

E-mail from God for Kids

TELL ME WHERE IT HURTS

He has sent me to bind up the brokenhearted.

| Isaiah | 61:1 |

My Child,

>I want to heal your heart. I want to heal the deep hurts and the hidden fears. I want to make you whole and healthy emotionally and spiritually. That's a pretty scary thought to lots of people. Some people spend their whole lives running from that healing. They'd rather keep the pain down inside, where they're used to it. They fear that healing will hurt them more than help them.

Well, real healing does hurt a little. When you have surgery, it hurts for a while afterwards. Things that weren't exposed have to come into the light and be set straight. But just like surgery, the healing that I want to do in your wounded heart will make you better than you were before.

So don't fear my healing. Open yourself to me. Tell me where it hurts. Tell me what or who hurt you. Ask me to heal your heart, and I will.

Your Healer,

God
=== =========

BRING ME THE WHOLE ORANGE

I am the good shepherd, and I know
My own and My own know me.

John   10:14 NASB

My Awesome Child,

>Have you ever noticed how you have to peel an orange to get to the good stuff inside? That's how it is when you get to know other people. Everyone has an outer shell, like an orange peel. It's the thing that protects them and guards who they are inside. It's the thing that helps them function in life.

Their outer peel might be grumpiness or shyness or even acting sweet all the time. And I'm not saying that the way they act on the outside is not a part of who they are. I'm just saying that the best stuff is found once you get past the shell.

Lots of people are content to spend their lives just knowing the outer peels of people. But that's not how I am. I want you to show me who you really are. I want to peel back that layer you keep on the outside and see who you really are inside. I want to know the deep, great stuff about you. I want to know the hidden, bad stuff too. I want all of who you are. So don't just bring me the outer peel; bring me the whole orange.

Looking for the Real Stuff,
God

=== =========

E-mail from God for Kids

COME DOWN OUT OF THE TREE

Truly, truly, I say to you, unless a grain of wheat falls into the earth and dies, it remains alone; but if it dies, it bears much fruit.

John   12:24 NASB

My Child,

>There could be the most perfect apple in the whole world growing on an apple tree. It could be perfectly red, beautifully shaped, deliciously sweet. But if that apple just hung there and ripened and rotted on the tree, it would be worthless. That's because an apple was meant to feed living creatures and to grow more apple trees from its seeds. If it doesn't do that, the reason for its existence is wasted.

In the same way, I haven't made you just for yourself. Your purpose in life isn't to try to look the best you can. It's to make a difference in your world, to make a difference in other people's lives. I have given you the ability to change the world for me. I have given you the ability to help feed others, both physically and spiritually. I have placed inside you the truth of Jesus Christ, and I want you to share that truth with other people. So don't just hang there on the tree looking good. Come on down and make a difference.

I'll help you change the world,

God

=== =========

JOIN THE REVOLUTION

As Jesus went on from there, he saw a man named Matthew sitting at the tax collector's booth. "Follow me," he told him, and Matthew got up and followed him.

| | Matthew | 9:9 | |

My child,

>Did you know that I want you be part of my revolution? A revolution is something that totally changes the way people look at things. I want to use your life to turn your world upside down. When people say, "You've got to look out for number one," I want you to tell them, "You've got to look out for others." When people look down on the misfits of life, I want you to treat them with kindness. When people want to just slide by, doing as little as they can, I want to help you to do amazing and miraculous things on the earth. When people are totally full of themselves, I want you to be filled with my Holy Spirit. Where there is hate and anger, I want you to bring my love. Where there is only hopelessness, I want you to bring the hope of Jesus Christ.

Jesus was the ultimate revolutionary. He changed everything for all times. And if you trust me, I'll make you a revolutionary too.

Your Leader,
God

E-mail from God for Kids

BIG THINGS FROM LITTLE PEOPLE

Then David said to the Philistine, "You come to me with a sword, a spear, and a javelin, but I come to you in the name of the Lord of hosts, the God of the armies of Israel, whom you have taunted."

 1 Samuel 17:45 NASB

My Child,

>You can do amazing things if you let me help you. Look at the shepherd boy David. He was small and inexperienced and weak compared to Goliath, the giant. Nothing on earth could have helped David defeat Goliath. But Goliath was trusting in his own size and strength to win that showdown, and David was trusting in me. With my help, that little boy wiped out that giant with one small stone. It was a direct hit to the head.

So what are the giants in your life? What are the things that you feel as if you just can't defeat? I want you to know that regardless of your size, your age, or your abilities, you can do great things. If you trust in me like David did, I will give you my power to overcome huge opponents and accomplish great things.

Trust in me,

God

=== ==========

EVEN THE SMALLEST THINGS

David girded his sword over his armor and tried to walk, for he had not tested them. So David said to Saul, "I cannot go with these, for I have not tested them." And David took them off. He took his stick in his hand and chose for himself five smooth stones from the brook, and put them in the shepherd's bag which he had, even in his pouch, and his sling was in his hand; and he approached the Philistine.

1 Samuel   **17:39–40** NASB

My child,

>When the little shepherd David went to face the giant Goliath, David didn't have the typical battle gear. King Saul had tried to dress him up in some fancy armor with a big sword, but that cramped David's style. There was Goliath, dressed in the most awesome battle gear, and what did David reach for? A laser gun? A nuclear missile? A donkey-powered tank? No. He reached down and picked up some small, round stones to put into his slingshot. That would be like you going up against a fully armed Green Beret with just a BB gun. But the ammunition that David chose to use wasn't as important as his faith in me.

That's true in your life too. Sometimes you will come up against some pretty hard stuff. And you may feel that you don't have much to fight with. But if you trust in me, I can use even the smallest things to help you get through. Your faith in me is what makes you a winner.

Trust in me,
God
=== =========

E-mail from God for Kids

I DON'T GIVE UP ON YOU

I tell you that you are Peter, and on this rock I will build my church, and the gates of Hades will not overcome it.

| Matthew | 16:18 |

My child,

>Do you ever feel like you don't measure up? Like you don't even have enough energy to keep your own life together, much less make a difference in other people's lives? Like you keep letting yourself and me down?
Well, you're in good company. Peter was a man who had all the best intentions, but he couldn't quite follow up. He was the one who stepped out and walked to Jesus on the water, but then he chickened out and started to sink. He boldly proclaimed that Jesus was the Christ, but then he told Jesus not to go to the cross. He was the one who said, "Even if everyone else leaves you, I won't leave you." But then he lied and said he didn't even know Jesus.

But did I give up on Peter? No way. He was the rock that I used to build my church. I used him to do mighty miracles and to be one of the first leaders of the church. So if I can use Peter, I can use you. Cut yourself some slack. You don't have to be perfect for me to use you, just willing. Don't give up on yourself, because I will never give up on you.

I believe in you,
God

=== ==========

DEALING WITH THE JERKS

Love your enemies, and do good to them, and lend to them without expecting to get anything back. Then your reward will be great, and you will be sons of the Most High, because he is kind to the ungrateful and wicked.

Luke	6:35

My Child,

>You may come across some pretty weird and obnoxious people in your life. These people may openly reject me and go against everything you believe in. You may find yourself wishing those difficult people would throw themselves off a tall cliff and be done with it.

But I want you to know something important. Behind every difficult person is a bunch of pain. They may have been hurt or wounded by things in their past. They may not understand who I really am. They may be afraid of the truth, and that may be making them mean. You never know what makes a person tick until you make an effort to find out.

I am calling you to love difficult people and help them find my healing. If someone is a jerk to you, don't be a jerk back. Take time to find out where that person is coming from. Try to reach out in some way. I know this may be hard. But I want you to love your enemies, not just because it's the "Christian thing to do." Love them because they need the love.

The One Who Loves Them,
God

E-mail from God for Kids

THE WAY OF MERCY

I say to you, do not resist an evil person; but whoever slaps you on your right cheek, turn the other to him also. If anyone wants to sue you and take your shirt, let him have your coat also. Whoever forces you to go one mile, go with him two.

Matthew	5:39-41 NASB

My Child,

>The Old Testament rules gave people permission to get even. If someone did something wrong to a person, they were allowed to do the same wrong thing back. But I sent Jesus to show people a better way. He taught that when someone slaps you on one cheek, you need to turn the other cheek.

That seems crazy, I know. If some jerk hits you, why should you give him a chance to hit you again? He should get what's coming to him, right? Well, not really. There's a better way—the way of mercy.

The way of mercy means forgiving others for hurting you. Turning the other cheek means being willing to lay down your pride and forgive. It means leaving room for making up. Instead of getting even, it means being humble. Instead of hating, it means loving. If you fight back just to give that jerk what he deserves, it will usually make him crazier. But if you show mercy and love, you may just see that person have a change of heart. I know it's a hard thing to do. But trust me. I'll help you take the way of mercy.

The Merciful One,
God

=== =========

HAVE MERCY

He was oppressed and afflicted, yet he did not open his mouth; he was led like a lamb to the slaughter, and as a sheep before her shearers is silent, so he did not open his mouth.

Isaiah 53:7

My child,

>What if someone you really loved accused you of all sorts of bad stuff that you didn't do? What if that person turned your friends against you with all sorts of lies and left you all alone? What if that person paid some thugs to beat you up and even got some crooked cops to arrest you for something you didn't do? Wouldn't that totally break your heart? It might even make you mad enough to want to get revenge.

Well, all of that happened to my Son, Jesus. It broke his heart to be betrayed by his friend and beaten by the people he came to save. But instead of getting even, he had mercy. One of the last things he said was, "Father, forgive them, because they don't know what they're doing."

In your life, if people are treating you badly or lying about you, know that you aren't alone. Jesus and I know how that feels. I can give you the strength you need to forgive instead of getting even. That's the way of Christ.

The One Who Has Mercy on You,

God

=== ==========

E-mail from God for Kids

Do not call to mind the former things,
or ponder things of the past.

Isaiah	43:18 NASB

My Child,

>There is one day in each week that you have absolutely
no control over. That day is yesterday. Do you spend a lot
of time worrying about things you did wrong in the past?
Do you ever play the could-have, should-have, would-have
game, wishing you could have done things differently?
Maybe you regret an argument and later you think, *I
should have said this or that.*

Well, worrying about yesterday is like trying to get on a
train that's already left the station. It doesn't do you any
good. Second-guessing yesterday is like trying to put icing
on a cake that's already been eaten. It's gone, and it isn't
coming back. If you've done something in the past that you
feel bad about, ask for my forgiveness and let it go. Instead
of spending a lot of time thinking about how you should
have done better, focus on doing it better today, right now.
Don't live your life in yesterday. Today is all you have.

The Here and Now,

God
===   =========

GUILT AND CONVICTION

Therefore repent and return, so that your sins may be wiped away, in order that times of refreshing may come from the presence of the Lord.

Acts 3:19 NASB

My Child,

>There is a huge difference between feeling guilty and being convinced you are wrong. Feeling guilty is like sitting around slapping yourself. It doesn't make you a better person. It just makes you think, *Oh, I'm no good. I might as well give up. What's the point in trying?* Satan loves to keep you feeling guilty because he doesn't want you to get right with me.

Being convinced you're wrong is feeling bad about what you've done and being motivated to get right with me. When you're convinced of your wrong, you want to turn away from the bad stuff and head towards doing good stuff. It makes you want to ask for and receive my forgiveness.

When you sin, I want to forgive you. I don't want you beating yourself up and saying, "Poor sinful me!" When you're wrong, come to me and say, "I sure did mess up, but now I'm ready to move on with you, God."

Let's move on,
God

=== ==========

E-mail from God for Kids

KNOW ME BETTER

That the God of our Lord Jesus Christ, the Father of glory, may give to you a spirit of wisdom and of revelation in the knowledge of Him.

Ephesians | **1:17 NASB**

My child,

>I am not some gray-bearded old man tucked away in an old folks' home. I am the strongest and most alive being in existence. I am not sitting around in a robe, riding on a donkey, and hoping one day someone will discover electricity. I know everything there is to know about the latest technology, and I even know all kinds of things that haven't been invented yet. I am not locked in a church, wearing a "preacher outfit," acting shocked at every bad thing in the world. I have seen every bad thing that can be done, and I've heard every bad word that can be said. I am sad about bad stuff, but nothing can shock me.

I am not a billion miles away, running the earth from my corporate offices in Heaven. I am as close as a whisper. I am not a drill sergeant, yelling at you to get your act together. I am a friend who wants the best for you. So get rid of all those wrong ideas about me. You can know me today. You can know me better than your best friend. And you can be exactly who I made you to be—the real you.

The Real Me,
God

=== ==========

LIGHT AND SALT

You are the light of the world.
A city on a hill cannot be hidden.

| Matthew | 5:14 |

My Child,

>I don't want you to live in a Christian bubble. Yes, I want you to have a strong support group of Christian friends who are pulling for you and praying for you. But if those are the only people you hang out with, then you aren't bringing light to my dark world.

When I lead you into a relationship with me, it's not just so you can sit around feeling good about yourself. When I save you, I have other people in mind. I have divine appointments that I want you to keep so that you can tell other people about my love, my goodness, and my saving power.

So if you find yourself in a Christian bubble, let me pop it. Move out into the world. Share my love with someone outside of your group of friends. I will use you to be a light to someone who needs it.

The One Who Sends You Out,

God

=== ==========

E-mail from God for Kids

*The goal of our instruction is love
from a pure heart and a good
conscience and a sincere faith.*

| | | | 1 Timothy | 1:5 NASB | | | | |

My Child,

>OK, pretend that you were the richest person in the world, and you fell in love with a not-so-rich person. Now how would you feel if that person didn't really love you back? What if he or she only came around to ask you for money and for things? Wouldn't that hurt your feelings and make you feel used?

That's exactly how I feel when you treat me that way. I love you tons, and I want you to love me back. But lots of times you only talk to me when you ask me for stuff. That's not a relationship; that's freeloading. I want you to come to me because you love me and want to spend time with me. I do want to bless you with all of my blessings, but I mostly just want you to know I love you. And I want you to love me back. So don't just ask for my riches; ask for me.

The One Who Loves You,

God

=== =========

I WANT TO BLESS YOU

The fruit of the Spirit is love, joy, peace, patience, kindness, goodness, faithfulness, gentleness, self-control. Against such things there is no law.

Galatians **5:22-23**

My child,

>It's easy to get the wrong idea about prayer. A lot of people think it's like an online shopping experience. They believe that if they pray to me for an expensive car, I should give it to them. That's not the way it works. If you asked me for a fancy car, and I knew that the car was just going to take your focus off of me and make you a prideful idiot, of course I wouldn't give it to you. That's because it wouldn't be the best thing for you. I will only give you stuff that will truly bless you. And things that will truly bless you aren't always top-dollar purchases.

The blessings that I want you to pray for are spiritual blessings, such as peace, joy, contentment, and being in a good relationship with me. These are the richest things you can hope to have. So don't get the wrong idea about prayer. It's not shop-online ordering time. It's a time of talking to me, a time of worship, and a time of looking for my best spiritual blessings.

The One Who Truly Blesses You,
God
=== ==========

E-mail from God for Kids

NO PAIN, NO GAIN

I am the Lord, your God, who takes hold
of your right hand and says to you,
Do not fear; I will help you.

| Isaiah | 41:13 |

My child,

>Even though the world you live in seems to say that you should avoid pain, that's not always true. Look at professional athletes. What if they slacked off and tried to avoid any pain in practice? By game time, they would be weaklings. Most professional athletes know that by pushing themselves and not shying away from the pain of hard work, they get to be the best at what they do.

The same is true with life. If you spend all of your time trying to avoid painful or difficult situations, then you aren't fully alive. If you avoid being yourself because people might laugh at you, then you aren't really living. If you run from hard work because it's unpleasant, then you will never find out what you're really capable of. That's not how I want you to live. I want you to be unafraid of the pain and the reality of life. I want you to know that I will see you through it all. Not only that, but I will use the tough things to make you stronger. Face the pain, and gain more life.

I'll see you through,

God

HIS PAIN, YOUR GAIN

Being found in appearance as a man, He humbled Himself by becoming obedient to the point of death, even death on a cross. For this reason also, God highly exalted Him, and bestowed on Him the name which is above every name.

Philippians **2:8-9 NASB**

My child,

>A hero isn't someone who sacrifices a little bit to save you. A real hero is willing to sacrifice everything he has, even his own life. That's exactly what Jesus did. He could have called on power from Heaven and blown away all the people who wanted to kill him. He could have played their political games and acted like the conquering king they wanted. He could have climbed down off the cross and walked away alive, but he didn't.

Because he knew that you needed a real hero and a Savior, he sacrificed himself. This was because with no sacrifice and death there would be no eternal life. Because of his death, Jesus made it possible for you to win against sin on earth and live forever in Heaven. So his pain and suffering became your gain and joy.

Your Father,

God

=== =========

E-mail from God for Kids

THE WEIGHT OF SIN

He himself bore our sins in His body on the cross, so that we might die to sin and live to righteousness; for by His wounds you were healed.

1 Peter 2:24 NASB

My Child,

>A sin is something you do that hurts someone else or yourself. A sin is knowing that something is wrong but choosing to do it anyway. Think of your sins like big, heavy rocks, one stacked on top of the other, and you have to hold all that weight over your head. Over time, the weight of your sin is bound to crush you. No other human can help you with your sin, because they are too busy holding up the weight of their own sin.

So what can you do? Call on Jesus, and he will help you. Because Jesus doesn't have any sin, he can come over and take your sin in his own hands and hold it up for you. He can even get rid of it. That's what happened on the cross. By taking your sin on himself, Jesus let you go free. That's good news for you. And he keeps on doing the same thing for you day after day.

Your forgiving Father,

God

LIFE IS NOT A SOLO PERFORMANCE

The one who is taught the word is to share all good things with the one who teaches him.

| Galatians | 6:6 NASB |

My Child,

>Have you ever watched the Academy Awards? The best and most famous actors in the world show up for the big night. Some are awarded prizes for their skill at making movies. But when they get up to receive the award, what do those stars do? They begin to thank the people in their lives who made it possible for them to do such a good job. What they are saying is, "Life is not a solo performance. Nobody gets to the top without lots of help."

And that's true of your life. If you are ever tempted to think that you're the best and you can do it all on your own, then it's time to start making a list of people who help you do well at what you do. Nobody succeeds all alone. So don't be prideful. Be thankful for all the help you've been given.

Your Helping Hand,

God
=== =========

E-mail from God for kids

Go and learn what this means: "I desire mercy, not sacrifice," for I have not come to call the righteous, but sinners.

 Matthew 9:13

My child,

>There are lots of good, churchgoing people who have a bad attitude about people who are different. They look down their noses at the ones they call "bad people"— people who make bad choices, people who live their lives outside of church, who dress weird or act strange.

Well, I want you to know a secret about these so-called bad people. They are just good people waiting to happen. Even if they really are choosing to live badly right now, that doesn't mean they have to stay that way. They may have made many bad choices, but I created every man and woman with tremendous potential for goodness. Most of them just need someone to believe in them and to reach out to them for me. I want you to believe in other people's potential for good.

People who don't know me don't need to be judged; they need to be loved. When you are tempted to look down on people who are making wrong choices, try praying for them instead. Pray that my love will bring out their goodness.

The compassionate One,
God

=== =========

THE CAR WITH THE ENGINE

For us there is but one God, the Father, from whom are all things and we exist for Him; and one Lord, Jesus Christ, by whom are all things, and we exist through Him.

| 1 Corinthians | 8:6 NASB |

My Child,

>There's a big, long word to describe the way some people in your modern world look at spiritual things. That word is "relativism." Relativism just claims that there is no real truth. It says one belief is as good as another.

But that doesn't make sense. Think about it this way. Suppose you were trying to get home, and you had a choice of three cars that could drive you there. All three look good on the outside, but only one of the three cars has an engine. It wouldn't matter what you believed about the three cars. Only the car with the engine could get you home.

The same is true about whom you choose to worship. You could worship a rock if you really wanted to. You could have all the faith in the world that that rock could get you to Heaven. But it wouldn't do you any good. Only one God has the power to get you there. I'm the one with the power. I am the way, the truth, and the life. Don't waste your time looking for "a truth." Look for the truth. When you do, you will find me.

The Truth,
God

E-mail from God for kids

DON'T BE A PACK RAT

Be kind to one another, tender-hearted, forgiving each other, just as God in Christ also has forgiven you.

| | | | | Ephesians | 4:32 NASB | | | | | |

My Child,

>Do you know someone who's a pack rat? A pack rat is someone who just can't seem to throw anything away? That person holds on to everything, thinking it may be useful one day. Pretty soon, that pack rat's room is bursting with junk.

Did you know that you can be an emotional pack rat? If you hold on to all your hurt feelings, your grudges, and your unfinished arguments, soon your heart will be bursting with pain and sadness. Or you will blow up with anger.

I don't want you to hold on to your anger or pain. I want you to let me help you take care of it. If someone has hurt you, come to me and talk to me about it. Give me the pain and let me heal you. If you feel like you still need to go to that person and talk about it, go. But go in love. In the end, I want you to forgive the ones who hurt you. Bring me all of your grudges, your hurt feelings, and your endless arguments. I'll help you clean out the closet of your heart.

Your Healer,
God
=== =========

LET IT FLOW

He who believes in Me, as the Scripture said, "from his innermost being will flow rivers of living water."

| John | 7:38 NASB |

My child,

>My love is like a river. I send it flowing through you and into other people's lives. Just like a river, my love can bring life wherever it flows. It can turn deserts into forests and someone's dry, mean heart into an alive, loving heart.

I'm always ready to send my love flowing through you, but sometimes your bad attitude builds a dam. If you choose to focus only on yourself, instead of caring about others, you block the flow of my love into your life.

But when you say, "Use me, Lord! Flow through me. Love other people through me," you open up the river channel, and my love flows freely. That's what I want for you. I want you to be wide open to what I am doing in your life, wide open to my loving you, and wide open to my love flowing through you to other people.

Let the river flow!

God

=== =========

E-mail from God for Kids

TOO SMART FOR YOUR OWN GOOD

Has not God made foolish the wisdom of the world? For since in the wisdom of God the world through its wisdom did not know him, God was pleased through the foolishness of what was preached to save those who believe.

| 1 Corinthians | 1:20-21 |

My child,

>Brilliant mathematicians and physicists are able to solve complex problems in math. Highly educated geneticists know all about the human genetic code. Skilled architects and engineers are able to build amazing structures. But even the smartest of these geniuses could make the dumbest mistake in the world. They could choose to reject the truth of my existence.

Because belief in me takes faith and not formulas, many people write it off as a myth. Because knowing me is a matter not just of the mind, but of the heart as well, it can confuse someone who understands head knowledge alone. I'm not against education or learning. I want you to study and reach your potential mentally. But I also want you to know me totally. Seek me with all of your mind, all of your heart, and all of your strength, and you will get to know me. Don't make the dumbest mistake in the world.

The Wisest of All,
God
=== =========

THE CROSS IS FOR TODAY

*Do not be afraid. Stand firm and you
will see the deliverance the Lord
will bring you today.*

Exodus **14:13**

My Child,

>When you think about my Son's crucifixion on the cross,
do you think about it as something that happened a long
time ago—something that has no importance to people of
today? If you think that way, then I want you to change
your thinking.

The cross matters to you today. Here's how: The cross is
like a love letter from me to you, not just telling you, but
showing you how much I love you. You can open that love
letter any time you think about the cross. The cross is like
a bridge from you to me. Because of the cross, you can
cross that bridge and talk to me anytime. The cross is like
a battery pack that can give you power to get through the
hard times, power to forgive others, and power to change
your world. The cross is like a multivitamin that gives you
the spiritual health you need to live your life to the fullest.

The cross is not just an ancient memory. It is an everyday
blessing to everyone who believes in me.

Your Father,
God

E-mail from God for Kids

I am with you and will watch over you wherever you go.

| | | | | | Genesis | 28:15 | | | | | |

My Child,

>I am here for you twenty-four hours a day, seven days a week. Don't think that I'm just sitting around at church, waiting for you to show up on Sunday. I am with you when you wake up in the morning. I am with you when you go to sleep at night. I hold you when you cry, and I laugh with you when you laugh. I am with you when you do your best, and I'm with you when you're at your worst. Because I love you, I will never leave your side, and you don't ever have to be alone again.

I am not hanging out judging you. I am hanging out loving you and helping you to be your best. So wake up to my reality in your life every day. I am with you right now. Talk to me. Let me talk to you. I will always be with you.

Your Friend,

God

=== ==========

I'M NOT TRYING TO BE COOL

Indeed Jews ask for signs and Greeks search for wisdom; but we preach Christ crucified, to Jews a stumbling block and to Gentiles foolishness, but to those who are the called, both Jews and Greeks, Christ the power of God and the wisdom of God.

1 Corinthians **1:22–24 NASB**

My child,

>I am not cool. I am not hip. And I am not trying to be either. If you are waiting for non-Christians to think that I am cool, then you'll be waiting a long time. People who want their own way don't think it's cool when I say to follow my way. People who want everything to make scientific sense think that a supernatural God is foolishness. People who love the latest, freshest thing are turned off by a God who's been around forever.

But the minute those people realize their need for something deeper in their lives, I will be here for them. The minute they are ready to put down the cool ideas of the modern world and look for me, they will find me. And once their eyes are open to me as I am, I will suddenly become the most amazingly cool thing they have ever seen. But until then, they won't catch on. So don't feel like you have to try to make me cooler than I am. Just believe in me and let me shine through your life. And pray that someday they'll see me the way you do.

Waiting to be known,
God

=== =========

E-mail from God for Kids

I KNOW THE ANSWER

Humble yourselves in the presence of the Lord, and He will exalt you.

| James | 4:10 nasb |

My Child,

>Have you ever had an argument with someone about the right answer to some question? You were positive your answer was right, and you even got mad at that other person for disagreeing with you. But later you found out that you were wrong all along. An experience like that can knock the wind out of your pride.

It is easy to go through life being prideful and thinking you know better than everyone else. But that is a horrible way to live. It can make you unpleasant to be around. It can even keep you from making friends.

I do want you to have confidence in your ideas and opinions. But I don't want you to be obnoxious about it. I want you to be humble. Admit when you're wrong. Keep disagreements from becoming arguments by using words like these: "I might be wrong about this, but I think I know the answer." When you're right, don't gloat over it. And when you're wrong, admit it. Make a real effort to be more humble. I will help you.

Your Father,

God

=== ==========

I'LL BE YOUR FATHER

A father to the fatherless, and a defender of widows, is God in his holy dwelling.

Psalm · 68:5

My child,

>If you have had a bad experience growing up with your earthly father, or if you've had no father at all, I know that it can be hard to picture me as a loving Father. But I am the Father to the fatherless. I am here to be the loving Dad that some people never had. I am here to love you like your earthly father could never love you.

So if "father" is a bad word to you, try calling me "heavenly Father" or even "Friend." If you will let me, I will be the Father that you need. I will be your strong protector, your provider, your biggest fan, and your best friend. I will be at every game, every school play, every high point and low point in your life, cheering you on. I am so proud of you, my child. Let me be your Father.

Your Heavenly Father,

God

=== =========

E-mail from God for Kids

STAND UP

He said, "Daniel, you who are highly esteemed, consider carefully the words I am about to speak to you and stand up, for I have now been sent to you." And when he said this to me, I stood up trembling.

Daniel **10:11**

My child,

>Have you ever seen one of those action movies where the hero gets shot at a billion times but never gets hit? But then when the hero shoots at the bad guys, he hits them every time. That might work in Hollywood, but if you want to be a real-life hero, you've got to be willing to take some shots. If you stand up for me and do my will, everything in hell will try to rise up against you.

Living the Christian life isn't easy, but it is the most action-packed way to live your life. If you will stand up and say, "I'll be your hero, God," then I will begin to use you to do amazing things. I will take you places you didn't think possible. I will help you accomplish the unbelievable. You may come under some attack along the way, but I will protect you and help you fight. You may not win every battle, but by living a life that matters, you will win the war. Stand up and be a hero for me.

Your Partner,

God

=== ==========

NO ONE CAN CUT THE LINE

Now I know that the Lord saves his anointed;
he answers him from his holy heaven with
the saving power of his right hand.

| Psalm | 20:6 |

My Child,

>Have you ever seen one of those scary movies where the bad guys break into a house and cut the phone line? When the homeowners try to call for help, the line is dead. And they are in deep trouble. That's what Satan tries to do through sin. He tries to sneak into your life and cut off your communication with me. If you feel like you can't call for help, then you probably won't even try.

But I want you to know that you can always call me for help. Because Jesus died and rose again, our line of communication can't be cut. So if you feel like you can't talk to me because of sin in your life, you're wrong. Just call to me; confess your sin; and ask me to throw Satan out. No one can keep us from talking to each other, ever.

Always Here,

God
=== ==========

E-mail from God for Kids

NEVER TOO BUSY

*If shall come about that when he cries out
to Me, I will hear him, for I am gracious.*

Exodus   **22:27 NASB**

My child,

>Have you ever tried to call a friend, but that friend's line
was busy? And if the phone stays busy for hours, it can
drive you crazy if you really need to talk.

Well, when you need to talk to me, I want you to know
that my line is never busy. Even though it may seem that
I've got a lot to do, I always have time for you. I am big
enough to do all I need to do. And I'm still available for
our time together.

So how do you make the call? By praying. Praying to me is
like placing a phone call to my private line. Just say, "Hey,
God, I want to talk to you." And then just start talking. Tell
me what's on your heart. Let's talk about all the stuff you
love to talk about. And let's talk about the things that I
want to say to you. I am the friend you can always count
on to hear your call and to answer you. Just give me a call
through prayer anytime.

Your friend,

God

===   =========

GUIDEBOOK TO A GOOD LIFE

I will meditate on Your precepts and regard Your ways. I shall delight in Your statutes; I shall not forget Your word.

 Psalm 119:15–16 NASB

My child,

>Did you know that the Bible has the secrets to living life to the fullest? It's not just a list of dos and don'ts meant to cramp your style. It is like a guidebook to the land of happy living.

Think about how much time you spend studying your math, history, and English books. That's good stuff, and it might come in handy one day. But the words of life in the Bible apply to your life right now, every day. Of course there's great stuff about salvation and eternity in there. But there is also practical, day-to-day advice on stuff like how to treat your friends, how to fight fair, how to date, and how to get the most out of your money.

So how much time do you spend studying the Bible? I don't want you to read the Bible so that you will look smart to your Sunday school teacher. I want you to read it because you need the stuff it teaches you about life and living. Look at the Bible as your personal guidebook to a better life.

The Author,
God

=== =========

E-mail from God for Kids

PLACE YOUR LIFE IN MY HANDS

Yet, O Lord, you are our Father. We are the clay, you are the potter; we are all the work of your hand.

| Isaiah | 64:8 |

My Child,

>Have you ever seen a beautiful piece of pottery, like a really cool vase or pot? The finished product looks perfect and may cost lots of money, but the guy or girl who made that pottery had to get dirty when making it. A potter starts by throwing some ordinary clay on a wheel that turns. There's no way to do it without getting your hands dirty. When it starts out, that pot looks like an old lump of clay. But with skill, patience, and a little imagination, that clay can become a wonderful work of art.

I am like the potter, and you are like the clay. Even if you feel like you keep messing up, and even if you don't see yourself as beautiful, it doesn't matter. I can see the awesome potential in you. If you place yourself and your life in my hands, I will make you into a perfect work of art. I will mold your character. I will develop your skills and gifts. I will lead you toward wholeness, completeness, and fulfillment. I love you. Place your life in my hands and watch your potential become beauty.

The Master Artist,
God
=== ==========

THE HARD TIMES

When they had struck them with many blows, they threw them into prison, commanding the jailer to guard them securely.... But about midnight Paul and Silas were praying and singing hymns of praise to God, and the prisoners were listening to them.

Acts   16:23,25 NASB

My Child,

>I don't always make your life easy. Sometimes I can use the hardest times in your life to mold you into the kind of person I want you to be.

If you wanted to carve a piece of wood into a certain shape, would you use a feather? No, you would use something sharp and hard that could chisel away the extra wood. If you allow yourself to be molded by me, even the hardest things can be blessings in your life. Your part in it is to trust me when hard times come.

I don't expect you to go through the hard times without feeling any pain. When something sad happens to you, you will cry, and you will feel it. But I will help love you through the pain. I will help you get through it without blaming others or feeling sorry for yourself. And when you move on to happier times, you'll look back and see how I used your struggles to mold you into a person of character.

The Molder of Your Character,
God

=== =========

E-mail from God for Kids

RISE TO THE CHALLENGE

*Be on the alert, stand firm in the faith,
act like [strong people], be strong.*

1 Corinthians | **16:13 NASB**

My Child,

>Challenges strengthen you. Think about it. If you had the ability to move, but you just lay in bed every day and watched television, your body would get flabby, and your mind would get weak. By getting out and facing the challenges of your day, you build your mental, physical, and spiritual muscles. You gain strength and stamina.

If you keep steering clear of difficult situations, you are avoiding the chance to grow and get stronger. Avoiding challenges is like crawling back into bed and switching the television on. It keeps you weak. So welcome the difficult challenges in your life, not as pains that you have to endure, but as opportunities for growth. That's the attitude that will make you strong.

Rise to the challenge,

God

=== =========

GO AND TELL!

When they had seen him, they spread the word concerning what had been told them about this child, and all who heard it were amazed at what the shepherds said to them.

Luke | 2:17-18

My Child,

>Suppose you had been one of the shepherds taking care of sheep in the desert on the night Jesus was born. They were probably pretty bored just sitting around. Then suddenly the whole sky blazed with light. Angels were singing about the birth of a new king who would bring peace to the whole world.

Wouldn't you have rushed to Bethlehem to see the newborn King with your own eyes? And once you had found him there, wouldn't you have wanted to tell everyone about him, just like the shepherds did?

Now think about this. If Jesus lives in your heart, don't you know him much better than those shepherds did? Then why aren't you telling everyone about what you have found? Go and tell!

Father of the Good News,

God
=== =========

E-mail from God for Kids

THE RIDE OF YOUR LIFE

You need to stick it out, staying with God's plan so you'll be there for the promised completion.

| | Hebrews | 10:36 | | |

My Child,

>Some people believe that putting their faith in me is like buying a ticket for a trip. They use it to get to the destination called "Saved." Then they get off the train and don't think any more about it.

The Christian life is not an earthly destination. It's a continuing journey with many stops along the way. I'm constantly moving you closer to me and drawing you into deeper levels of understanding. As long as you're alive, you'll be changing and growing and learning new things. So hang on to your ticket of faith and stay on the train. This is the ride of your life!

The Train Conductor,

God

=== =========

ALL THINGS ARE POSSIBLE

*I tell you the truth, if you have faith as small as
a mustard seed, you can say to this mountain,
"Move from here to there," and it will move.
Nothing will be impossible for you.*

Matthew   17:20

My Child,

>Some people let other people tell them what they are
capable of doing. They settle for less in their lives because
a parent told them they would never amount to anything.
Other people spend their whole lives chasing their
parents' dreams, rather than finding out what I want them
to do.

If you know me, you aren't limited by what people say
you can or can't do. You aren't bound by what you think
your gifts and abilities are. With me in your life, you have
no limitations. You can do anything I call you to do. If you
feel like I'm telling you to do something that is too huge
or impossible, don't worry. You won't have to do it on
your own. I will be with you every step of the way. So
don't be afraid to ask me for a huge plan for your life.
Through me, all things are possible.

The Possibility-maker,

God
=== =========

E-mail from God for Kids

I LOVE TO GIVE YOU GOOD STUFF

Now suppose one of you fathers is asked by his son for a fish; he will not give him a snake instead of a fish, will he?

Luke 11:11 NASB

My Child,

>Pretend that you were the richest person in the world. Now pretend that you fell in love with someone who was very poor. Wouldn't you want to meet that person's needs? Wouldn't you have a great time giving that person really good things because of your love? Of course you would.

That is how I feel about you. I own everything on earth—all the stuff is mine. And I love you totally. So you don't have to worry about me giving you what you need. It makes me happy to provide for you. Maybe it's not money you need. Maybe you need strength to get through each day. Maybe you need the salvation of my Son, Jesus Christ. Maybe you need healing or help with a relationship. Whatever your need is, trust me to provide for you.

The One with the Wealth,

God
=== ==========

NO EXCUSES

They all alike began to make excuses. The first one said to him, "I have bought a piece of land and I need to go out and look at it; please consider me excused."

Luke 14:18 NASB

My child,

>It's so tempting to make excuses. When you come in second, it's tempting to say, "If I had just had my good running shoes, I would have won." When you treat somebody mean, it's tempting to say, "Well, if he hadn't yelled at me the other day, I wouldn't have been so mean."

But I don't want you to live your life in this land of excuses. I want you to trust me, to do your level best at everything you do, and to accept the results with no excuses. I want this for you because people who live their lives making excuses for everything never find out who they really are. They hide their mistakes and brag about their abilities. But until you know your real strengths and weaknesses, you don't know yourself. So put on your best running shoes, get in there, and do the best you can. No excuses!

Your Father,

God

=== =========

E-mail from God for Kids

ONE BITE AT A TIME

*I gave you milk, not solid food, for you
were not yet ready for it. Indeed,
you are still not ready.*

1 Corinthians **3:2**

My Child,

>I don't expect you to be a spiritual giant overnight. You have a whole life of walking with me ahead of you. And I will give you exactly what you need at every step to make you into the person I want you to be.

When you were a baby with no teeth, your mom didn't give you steak to eat. She knew you weren't ready for it; so she started you on milk. In the same way, I will grow you up spiritually one stage at a time. Don't get frustrated if you aren't a mature Christian yet. I'm working on that. Just stay hungry for spiritual things. Let yourself be fed through Bible study, prayer, worship, teaching, and friendships with other Christians. And I will cause you to grow up to be a mighty child of my kingdom. Let's just take it one bite at a time.

The One Who Feeds You,

God

=== =========

DON'T QUESTION THE PILOT

Woe to the one who quarrels with his Maker--an earthenware vessel among the vessels of earth! Will the clay say to the potter, "What are you doing?" Or the thing you are making say, "He has no hands"?

Isaiah 45:9 NASB

My Child,

>When you're flying on an airplane, you don't question the pilot about how he's flying the plane. When you feel a little turbulence, you don't go knock on the cockpit door and tell him you're going to take over. No. You trust that the pilot knows what he's doing.

In the same way, I want you to trust me with your life. It's easy to say, "Take my life, Lord, and do with it as you please." But when things aren't going the way you think they should, it's tempting to say, "Thanks, God. I'll take over from here."

If you had plans to be a lawyer and I called you to be a missionary, you might be tempted to go to law school anyway. Or if you had plans to be a preacher and I called you to be an engineer instead, you might be tempted to go to seminary anyway. But you need to know that when you put me at the controls of your life, I know what is best. I have steered billions of people through wonderful lives that they could never have dreamed up on their own. Trust me to do the same for you.

The Pilot of Your Life,
God
=== ==========

E-mail from God for Kids

YOUR SOLID FOUNDATION

For no one can lay any foundation other than the one already laid, which is Jesus Christ.

| 1 Corinthians | 3:11 |

My Child,

>You could build the coolest house in the world. It could even be made of solid gold. But if that house didn't have a solid, strong foundation, it would come crashing down. The foundation is the very bottom of a house, the part that supports everything else.

Jesus Christ is the solid foundation on which you can build an awesome life. You have to base your life on something. If you choose to build on him and his truth, no dream will be too big, no problem will be too big. But if you choose to build your life and your self-worth on earthly things, like money, looks, or success, it is all bound to come crashing down someday. Money, looks, and success aren't bad, but they were never meant to hold up your whole life. Only Jesus can be your solid foundation.

Your Father,

God

=== =========

GO FOR IT!

This was in accordance with the eternal purpose which He carried out in Christ Jesus our Lord, in whom we have boldness and confident access through faith in Him.

 **Ephesians** | **3:11-12** NASB

My child,

>It is easy to be an expert while you're watching from the sidelines. It's easy to say, "I could do that." It's easy to live your life playing it safe, making sure you don't mess up. But I'd rather have one person who tries and messes up than a million people who don't try at all.

I want you to be that one person who tries. Don't live your life protecting yourself from failure. Live your life going for the absolute best I have for you, and don't settle for less. If you feel like I'm calling you to do something really hard, don't sit around figuring out the reasons why you can't make it work. Get out there and do it. You may not totally succeed, but if you don't risk anything, you won't accomplish anything. Don't live your life playing it safe. Step out and trust me.

Then go for it!

God

=== ==========

E-mail from God for Kids

WHAT AN OPPORTUNITY

*You have made known to me the paths
of life; you will fill me with joy in your presence.*

| Acts | 2:28 |

My Child,

>When you wake up in the morning, what's the first thing
you think about? Are you excited about your day, or do
you roll out of bed thinking, *Oh boy, here we go again?*

If you dread going through another day, then you need an
attitude change. I want you to be able to look at life as an
adventure, not as a dead-end street. Even if it seems like
you go through the same routine every day (school,
homework, television, bed), you can still wake up to the
beauty of life. If you can begin to look at each day as an
amazing, once-in-a-lifetime opportunity, then you will
really begin to love life.

Each day is totally unique, filled with chances to love
others, chances to hear amazing things from me, chances
to experience life. I want you to look for the beautiful
things about your life. They are there, even if you aren't
noticing them yet. Open your eyes and start to see life as
an opportunity rather than a dull routine.

Making Each Day Awesome,

God

=== =========

WATCH OUT FOR THE NEGATIVE

I am afraid that perhaps when I come I may find you to be not what I wish and may be found by you to be not what you wish; that perhaps there will be strife, jealousy, angry tempers, disputes, slanders, gossip, arrogance, disturbances.

2 Corinthians 12:20 NASB

My Child,

>Negative people are like heavy weights that drag you down. Whenever you hang around people who look at life as one big hassle, it's hard to avoid their way of thinking. If the friends you hang out with are always putting people down, it's almost contagious. Pretty soon, you're joining in.

I have an assignment for you today. I want you to notice how much of what your friends say and do is negative. Don't judge them for their negative attitudes, and don't preach to them. I just want you to notice. And as you're noticing, try to keep from joining in with your own negative comments. Sometimes you can get so used to being around negative stuff that it seems normal. But I want you to see people through eyes of love. And I want you to see life as wonderful and positive.

Your Father,

God
=== =========

E-mail from God for Kids

THE HURT OF GOSSIP

You shall not go about as a slanderer among your people, and you are not to act against the life of your neighbor; I am the Lord.

| Leviticus | 19:16 NASB |

My child,

>Have you ever heard anyone saying something bad about you? Didn't it hurt your feelings? Gossiping, or talking bad about other people, is such an easy habit to fall into. It can be funny, or it can just be something to talk about when there's nothing else to say. But gossip hurts people. It hurts the person who's being talked about, and it also hurts the person who is talking. If you are the one talking bad, it is hurting your heart, because I made you to love others, not hurt them.

So before you start talking behind somebody's back, I want you to imagine saying those things to that person's face. And before you say something bad to someone's face, imagine how you would feel if someone said that to you. Think about what you're doing with your words. Don't hurt other people, and don't hurt yourself.

Your father and friend,

God

=== =========

AWKWARD STAGE?

Remember these things, O Jacob, for you are my servant, O Israel. I have made you, you are my servant; O Israel, I will not forget you.

Isaiah 44:21

My child,

>When people start to mature, funny things can happen. Maybe you're seeing some of those changes in yourself. Your voice may squeak when it's changing. You may grow tall and become a little clumsier than you were before. You may get so many pimples that it looks like the pizza man made a delivery to your face. You may gain or lose some weight. When these kinds of things are happening, it can seem weird because it's like you are not the person you were before. It can seem as if you're wearing a whole new body, and it doesn't seem to fit.

If you feel this way, I want you to know how much I love you. Even if it seems that you're in an awkward stage, I see you as perfect. I am growing you up, and anything that ends up beautiful has to go through some changes. If you walk with me, I will take you through the awkward stages with grace and style. You're my kid. I love you just the way you are.

Your Father,
God
=== =========

E-mail from God for Kids

DON'T TRASH THE HOUSE

Don't you know that you yourselves are God's temple and that God's Spirit lives in you?

1 Corinthians **3:16**

My child,

>If you built a million-dollar house on an awesome piece of land, I bet you wouldn't go dump a bunch of trash on the floor and throw mud and rotten food all over the walls. Instead, you would want to decorate it with the best stuff you could afford.

Well, you are the priceless house where my Son and my Holy Spirit and I will make our home, if you will let us. I want to furnish your life with only the finest and most beautiful things, such as love, purity, and kindness. These things will make your life a place of beauty and comfort. But choosing to focus on things like lust, impurity, or hate is exactly like trashing your life. It's like dumping garbage on newly finished floors and throwing mud on newly painted walls. I made you for all the good stuff, my child. Don't trash your life.

Your Builder,

God

=== =========

A NEW PERSON

If is not what you and I do. . . . If is what God is doing, and he is creating something totally new, a free life!

Galatians 6:14–15 | THE MESSAGE

My Child,

>When you ask me into your life, I make you a new person. It's not that I make you into some sort of Christian robot clone. What I do is make you the best you can be.

I take eyes that might have looked hopelessly at life, and I replace them with eyes that see life with hope. I take a mouth that might have spoken angry, hurtful words and replace it with a mouth that speaks words of love and healing. I take hands that worked for selfish things and replace them with hands that lift me up and serve others. I take a broken, bitter heart and replace it with a heart of forgiveness and freedom. If you ask me to, I will give you this new life and make you into this new person.

The One Who Can Change You,

God

=== ==========

E-mail from God for Kids

UNLOCK THE DOOR—IT'S ME

Here I am! I stand at the door and knock. If anyone hears my voice and opens the door, I will come in and eat with him, and he with me.

Revelation	3:20

My Child,

>I am standing at the door of your heart and knocking. I want to come into your life and be the best friend you ever had. I want to give you an amazing life on earth and an eternity in Heaven. But you are the one who has to open up and let me in. I am not going to break down the door of your heart and make you love me. So are you ready to open up, or are there things that are blocking the entrance?

What are the locks on the door of your heart? Are you scared of what might happen if you open up to me? Are you angry at me about something that has gone wrong in your life? Do you feel like you are too sinful to let me come in? Or do you just not understand why the God of the universe would want to come into your heart?

Well, whatever is locking up your heart, I encourage you to turn the key and throw the door open. I'm asking you to give me a chance. If you will, you'll find that you don't have to be afraid. I will come in and bring the forgiveness and the friendship you need. Open the door of your heart and let me in.

Your friend,
God
=== =========

LET ME FLY YOUR LIFE

The Lord will guide you always.

| Isaiah | 58:11 |

My Child,

>If you had to sit down in the seat of a navy jet plane and take off, whom would you choose to sit in the cockpit with you and help you fly? Would you choose your best friend or your neighbor or your teacher? Probably not. If you didn't want to crash, you would choose the best pilot you could find. You would search for someone who knows everything there is to know about that plane.

Well, your life is a little bit like a trip in a complicated jet plane. Your friends and neighbors and teachers may offer you some well-meaning advice. But no one on earth can handle the "plane" of your life as well as the one who designed it. Since I am the creator of life, I am the best pilot life has to offer. Don't try to fly alone, and don't settle for a second-rate pilot. Place your life in my hands, and I will steer you to amazing places.

Your Life-pilot,

God
=== ==========

E-mail from God for Kids

In this case, moreover, it is required of stewards that one be found trustworthy.

| 1 Corinthians | 4:2 NASB |

My Child,

>In the Bible, a steward is not someone who serves drinks and pretzels on an airplane. A steward is someone who takes care of someone else's stuff. A steward takes care of his boss's belongings and tries to do a good job of it. What can really mess stewards up is when they start to believe that the stuff they are taking care of really belongs to them. That's when they get selfish and start doing a horrible job.

You are my steward on the earth. I am the creator and owner of the earth and everything on it, and that includes your life. One of the worst mistakes you can make is to believe that your life and the things in it are totally your own. I have given you great gifts and a lot of responsibility. It's up to you to choose how you will manage your life. I hope that you will use it for good. I hope you will live unselfishly and use all that you've been given to honor me.

The Owner of Everything,
God

=== =========

WILLINGNESS

Mary said, "Behold, the bondslave of the Lord; may it be done to me according to your word."

Luke **1:38 NASB**

My child,

>When the angel appeared to the virgin Mary and told her that she was going to become the mother of my Son, think about how she must have felt. That's some pretty wild news! Out of all the women in the world, she had been chosen to have my Son!

Mary didn't know all the details of how that would happen or how it would change her life, but she suddenly had a choice to make. She could either choose to go along with my plan for her life or say no and let me pass her by.

Though Mary didn't have any money and she wasn't even married yet, she did have a huge gift. Mary had faith. She was willing to do what I asked. She basically said, "Go ahead and use me, God, however you want. I want to be a part of your plan."

By being willing, Mary was letting me use her life to change the world forever. I want you to have the same willingness Mary had. When I show you my plan for your life, I want you, like Mary, to say, "Go ahead and use me, God."

Be willing!

God

=== ==========

E-mail from God for Kids

LIKE A SONG

You formed my inward parts; You wove me in my mother's womb. I will give thanks to You, for I am fearfully and wonderfully made; wonderful are Your works, and my soul knows it very well.

Psalm 139:13–14 NASB

My Child,

>When a songwriter writes a great song, it is a labor of love. That song is created with just the right words, the perfect chords, and a melody that makes it all work great. Sometimes the songwriter will be amazed at his or her own song because it turned out so great.

That's how I feel about you. When I created you, I worked at it. I didn't randomly pick what kind of person I was making. It really mattered to me. I picked out the perfect mind for you. That doesn't mean it is the smartest mind in the world or the most creative; it's simply the perfect one for you. I also picked out a great body for you. And even though you might sit there and notice every imperfection, I knew what I was doing when I put you together. And I put it all together with a winning spirit. That's like your heart, your personality, your "you-ness."

When I see you, I am amazed at my own work. I couldn't be more proud of you, my child. I want you to begin to see my art in you and know how much I love you.

Your Father,
God
=== =========

PLAY AS A TEAM

But the one who joins himself to the Lord is one spirit with Him.

 1 Corinthians　6:17 NASB

My child,

>You could join the soccer team at your school or local park. You could pay the money, get the uniform, attend the practices, and go to all the games. But unless your team learned how to play as a team, they'd lose every game. You see, there is a difference between just *being* on a team and really *playing* as a team.

The same is true about your faith. If you believe in Jesus and me, and if you ask us to come into your life, then you've joined the Christian team. But you still have choices to make every day. Are you going to join with me and play on my team in this game called life? Are you going to ask me every day for the game plan? Are you going to go all out to work with me and your Christian teammates for the best life has to offer? Or are you going to just keep doing your own thing and lose the game? I'm encouraging you. Don't be just a team member. Join with me every day, and let's play as a team.

Your coach,
God
=== ==========

E-mail from God for Kids

APPLES, ORANGES, AND OTHER GOOD THINGS

Every good and perfect gift is from above, coming down from the father of the heavenly lights, who does not change like shifting shadows.

| | James | | 1:17 | | | |

My child,

>There are lots of people who live in big cities who will never see an apple tree or an orange tree. But they will go to their grocery store every week and buy apples and oranges. They will live their whole lives eating the fruit without ever seeing where it comes from.

In the same way, some people will live their whole lives enjoying all the beauty of this world. They will see my art in the beautiful sunsets. They will feel my kindness in the smile of a friend. They will feel my compassion in the care of a loved one. They will enjoy the fruit of my love, but they will never know me. That breaks my heart.

Everything good on earth is meant to be enjoyed, but it is also meant to point to me. I want you to be someone who enjoys all the good fruit of this life, but I also want you to know me, the giver of all good things.

Your father,

God
=== =========

GRAVITY AND GOD

He is before all things, and in Him
all things hold together.

Colossians 1:17

My child,

>Gravity is an invisible force that holds you and everything around you to the earth. It's the thing that keeps you from falling up through the ceiling when you wake up in the morning. It's the thing that allows you to move around without floating up into the air. You can't see gravity, but the effects of gravity are plain to see all around you.

In some ways, I'm a lot like gravity. I am a powerful force that allows you to live your life every day. I am here to keep you from floating away into a meaningless life. I help you move around confidently. You can't see me with your eyes, but you can see me working in the world all around you. Without me and without my presence on earth, everything would break into craziness. I hold things together. So don't doubt that I exist just because you can't see me. Just like gravity, I'm holding your world together.

Your Powerful Force,

God

=== ===========

E-mail from God for Kids

DON'T SLACK ON THE DETAILS

When she could hide him no longer, she got him a wicker basket and covered it over with tar and pitch. Then she put the child into it and set it among the reeds by the bank of the Nile.

Exodus   2:3 NASB

My Child,

>I don't want you to slack on the details in life. Sometimes things that don't seem important at all end up being very important.

Take Moses for instance. I used him to part the Red Sea in two. This was a hugely important event in history. Moses and the Israelites were able to cross from Egypt to the other side of the sea on dry land and were delivered from slavery.

But years earlier, when Moses was just a baby, his mother set him afloat in a basket in the Nile River to keep him from being killed. The way Moses' mother waterproofed his basket was a small detail compared to parting an entire sea, but it was just as important in achieving my plans for the Israelites. That basket carried Moses safely to where he was found by Pharaoh's wife, and it enabled him to live. If the basket had sunk and he had drowned, he never would have been alive to part the Red Sea.

In your life, I want you to be faithful in the small details as well as in the big events. Those little things can have a big impact on your life.

Helping with the Details,

God

=== ==========

OPEN UP

Therefore openly before the churches,
show them the proof of your love and
of our reason for boasting about you.

  2 Corinthians 8:24 NASB

My Child,

>No one would go to the trouble of building a nice, big house and then just board up all of the doors and windows. That would be crazy, because a house is meant to be enjoyed by the owner and his guests.

You are like an awesome house that I have built. There are so many great things about you that I want you to share with others. But if you close yourself off, then no one will be able to enjoy you. Don't be afraid to be yourself, and don't let shyness keep you closed off from others. Don't be afraid to invite other people to know you and to see me in your life. Open up and be the person I've created you to be. Let everyone see why I'm so proud of you.

Your Builder,

God

=== =========

E-mail from God for Kids

DON'T JUMP INTO SIN

*So, if you think you are standing firm,
be careful that you don't fall!*

1 Corinthians **10:12**

My Child,

>There once was a fast-food restaurant that had one of those big playgrounds with the ball pit and the slides and the tunnels. The ball pit was full of those colorful, plastic balls that you can slide and jump into. But one day after it had rained, some kids jumped into the ball pit to play, and they were bitten by some snakes that had made their home in the bottom of the balls. That was a dangerous awakening for those kids. What seemed to be fun had hurt them.

A lot of times sin can be a lot like that ball pit. It can look like lots of fun on the surface, but when you get down into it, you find out that it can bite you badly. Things like doing drugs can look like a lot of fun at first, but once you get involved, it can begin to wreck your life. So don't get lured in by sin that seems harmless and fun. Be sure to pray and be aware of the danger that lies beneath.

The One Who Protects You,

God

=== =========

NO FREEDOM

*All things are lawful for me, but not all things
are profitable. All things are lawful for me,
but I will not be mastered by anything.*

 1 Corinthians   6:12 NASB

My Child,

>If you were lost in a wild jungle and were trying to get
to safety, would you want to have the freedom to wander
around wherever you pleased? Or would you want to
know the best way to survive and escape?

If you had a guide who showed you the best way to go,
would you be angry at him? Of course you wouldn't. And
you would be glad when he warned you to stay away
from dangerous places. You'd be thankful when he
guided you toward the safest path.

Many times Christianity gets a bad rap. Some people think
it's a bunch of rules and regulations that keep people
from having any real fun. But that's not true. It is simply
the best path for you to walk through life. I am the guide
who warns you about hurtful things to stay away from.
And I tell you the way you should follow. You still have
the freedom to choose anything you want, but I want you
to choose the best things. Freedom with no guidance is no
freedom at all.

Your Guide,
God

===   ==========

E-mail from God for Kids

FORGIVE YOURSELF

Praise the Lord . . . who forgives all your sins.

| Psalm | 103:2 |

My child,

>Have you ever done something really dumb? Like maybe you said the wrong answer in class and everyone laughed at you. Now every time you think about that wrong answer, you feel embarrassed all over again.

In your mind, you keep saying mean things to yourself like, "You jerk, you dummy! Why didn't you just keep your big mouth shut?"

Sometimes it's easier to forgive other people than it is to forgive yourself. When you keep feeling guilty for past mistakes, you are refusing to forgive yourself. I'm the God of the whole universe, and I've already forgiven you; so shouldn't you forgive yourself? You'll do better next time.

The One Who forgives,

God

=== =========

YOUR LIFE IS YOUR SERMON

Do not merely listen to the word, and so deceive yourselves. Do what it says.

James   **1:22**

My child,

>Have you ever heard a preacher or a youth pastor preach an awesome sermon? Maybe his or her words even changed your life in some way. I love a good sermon, but I'm more interested in what happens when preachers stop talking and go back to living their lives. Will their actions match their words?

Jesus was an awesome preacher whose actions always matched his words. In fact, you can learn his lessons by looking at his life. Seeing him wash the feet of his friends, you learn to be a servant. Seeing him with his arms around little children, you learn to love. Seeing him on the cross forgiving his enemies, you learn to forgive. The most amazing sermon Jesus ever preached was the life he lived.

Let your actions match your words,

God
=== =========

E-mail from God for kids

As for God, his way is perfect;
the word of the Lord is flawless.

	2 Samuel	22:31	

My child,

>After you make a mistake, do you ever say, "Well, nobody's perfect"? Next time you open your mouth to make that statement, stop and think. That statement is not true.

Somebody is perfect, and I'm that Somebody. Everything about me is 100 percent right, true, and without fault. My ideas are perfect. My plans are perfect. My words are perfect. And here's the interesting thing. Everything I've created is perfectly created. That means you. Sure, sin can come along and mess with my perfect creation, but Jesus died to forgive you. And as soon as you confess your sins, I give you perfect forgiveness.

So next time you want to say "nobody's perfect," remember this. I am perfect, and I'm doing my perfect work in you.

The Perfect One,

God

=== =========

BIRDS, FISH, KANGAROOS, AND YOU

*We confidently and joyfully look forward
to actually becoming all that God has
in mind for us to be.*

| | Romans | 5:2 TLB | |

My Child,

>Have you ever watched a bird soaring through the air?
Birds make flying look so easy. Do you know why?
Because to a bird, flying is easy. Birds were created to fly.

Any time a creature is doing what it was created to do, it
won't be a struggle. Fish can swim underwater and never
come up for air. Kangaroos can hop for miles and not get
tired. Possums can rest while hanging by their tails.

Once you are doing what you were created to do, your life
will begin to feel easier and more fun than ever before.
You were created to love and trust me. You were created
to love other people and make a difference in your world.
Let me help you be the person I created you to be.

Your creator,

God

=== ==========

E-mail from God for kids

COOLER THAN VIDEO GAMES

Follow the way of love and eagerly desire spiritual gifts.

| 1 Corinthians | 14:1 |

My Child,

>Suppose you got a call from a guy at your local video store. And suppose he told you that the store had a free gift for you—five of the latest video games. You'd probably be pretty excited. But those video games wouldn't really be yours until you went down to the store and picked them up, would they?

I have free gifts for you too. My gifts are cooler than video games. I have secrets I want to share with you. I have an awesome plan for your life. I have love, forgiveness, and friendship. I have help for your problems and healing for your pain. So don't wait. Come to me and unwrap all the great stuff that's got your name on it.

The Gift-giver,

God

=== =========

THE CELEBRATION

The kingdom of heaven is like a king who prepared a wedding banquet for his son.

Matthew 22:2

My child,

>Imagine a huge celebration. A beautiful home is decorated with flowers and candles. There's music playing in every room. Delicious food is set out on big tables. The host stands at the door, happily greeting his guests. The rooms are filled with the sounds of talking and laughter.

My love is like a celebration that has already begun. I have sent out invitations to everyone. Some people are too busy to come. Some have to take care of business. Some would rather just stay home and watch television.

But lots of people are already at the party with me. They are enjoying the music, the laughter, and the friendship. Your invitation has already been sent. Will you come?

The Host,

God

=== =========

E-mail from God for kids

Now the Lord is the Spirit, and where the Spirit of the Lord is, there is freedom.

	2 Corinthians	3:17	

My child,

>Butterflies are some of the coolest things in my creation. Their wings are like tiny works of art created in many different colors and patterns. Butterflies don't have any special flight pattern like birds do. They just kind of do their own thing. They flutter and float along with total freedom.

But butterflies don't start out so colorful and free. They start out as drab caterpillars crawling through the dirt. They spend a long time wrapped in a cocoon, where they grow and change.

Don't be impatient if you sometimes feel as drab as a caterpillar. Remember, every butterfly starts out that way. Let me work in your life, and I'll transform you into someone who is beautiful and free!

Your cocoon,

God

=== ==========

A STORY OF TWO FATHERS

The Lord himself ... will be with you; he will never leave you nor forsake you.

	Deuteronomy	31:8	

My child,

>Once a man tried to make his daughter happy by giving her things. He worked long hours to afford expensive clothes and video games and the finest computer. But the girl was never happy.

Then one weekend the girl spent the night with a new friend. She was surprised to see the small, plain house her new friend lived in. There was no computer, no fancy clothes or games. But her friend's father was home early to fix dinner for the two girls. He talked and laughed with them during dinner, and the girl had a wonderful time. Sadly, she realized that her own father had given her many things, but he had never given her his time.

I've given you many gifts, my child, but the best gift I have for you is my time. Let me spend it with you.

Your Dad,

God

=== ==========

E-mail from God for Kids

NEW AND POWERFUL WORDS

You will be called by a new name
that the mouth of the
Lord will bestow.

| Isaiah | 62:2 |

My child,

>There's a little rhyme that says, "Sticks and stones can break my bones, but words will never hurt me." That just isn't true. Mean words hurt. When parents call their child "clumsy" or "worthless," it's almost like they are shooting him with a sharp arrow. When classmates call a kid "stupid" or "ugly," it hurts worse than a slap. Mean words stick like glue. But my love can wash them away. My love can pull out every mean name that has pierced you like an arrow.

Listen. I am speaking new and powerful words to you. I am giving you new names. You are Confident, Wise, and Gifted. You are Wonderful, Faithful, a Leader. Most of all, you are Mine.

The One Whose Words Are Truth,

God

=== =========

HOLD YOUR LIFE UP TO THE LIGHT

I am the light of the world.

| | John | 9:5 | |

My Child,

>Have you ever held a kaleidoscope up to the light and looked through the tiny peephole? The sparkling, colorful patterns look like jewels. But the truth is, they are nothing more than broken glass. It's the light shining through them that makes them beautiful.

Your life is a little bit like that kaleidoscope. When your plans don't work out, when your feelings get hurt, or when your hopes get smashed, your heart can feel as broken as that glass. But I am the God of new beginnings. Hold your life up to the light of my love. Let me shine through the broken, scattered pieces of your heart. I will pull those pieces together and create something beautiful and new in your life.

The Light,

God

=== =========

References

About the Authors

An award-winning lyricist, popular writer, and sought-after speaker, Claire Cloninger is one of the country's foremost Christian communicators. She is a six-time Gospel Music Association Dove Award winner whose Christian songs have been widely recorded by such artists as Amy Grant, Sandi Patti, and Wayne Watson. She has written more than two dozen musicals for church choir, including *My Utmost for His Highest* and *Experiencing God.*

Claire's inspirational books include *E-Mail from God for Teens, More E-Mail from God for Teens, A Place Called Simplicity, Simple Joys, When the Glass Slipper Doesn't Fit,* and *Postcards from Heaven.*

Claire holds a B. A. and an M. A. in Education from the University of Louisiana in Lafayette, where she was named Outstanding Alumna in 1991. Her teaching skills are put to good use in her national ministry as an inspirational speaker and retreat leader.

Claire and her husband, Robert, an artist, reside in a log home on the banks of a river in Alabama. They are active members of Christ Anglican Church, where he is a member of the Evangelism Committee and she serves on the Parish Prayer Team. They are the parents of two grown sons and grandparents of two granddaughters and one grandson.

Andy Cloninger, Claire's son, has a heart for meeting people where they are and loving them into the truth.

He is currently the contemporary worship leader at Spanish Fort United Methodist Church and plays professionally with the acoustic band Dog Named David. He also produces CDs for various bands and leads worship for youth events. Prior to beginning his musical career, Andy and his wife, Jenni, were youth ministers and worked with Young Life Ministries for several years.

Andy, Jenni, and their two children, Kaylee and Drew, make their home in Mobile, Alabama.

If you have enjoyed this book,
or if it has impacted your life,
we would like to hear from you.
Please contact us at:

RiverOak Publishing
Department E
P.O. Box 700143
Tulsa, Oklahoma 74170-0143

Additional copies of this book and other titles in the *E-mail from God* series are available from your local bookstore.

E-mail from God for Teens
More E-mail from God for Teens
E-mail from God for Men
E-mail from God for Women
E-mail from God for Teens screensaver

RIVER OAK

PUBLISHING